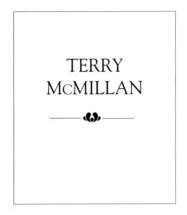

TERRY
McMILLAN

TERRY McMILLAN

Bruce & Becky Durost Fish

CHELSEA HOUSE PUBLISHERS
Philadelphia

Dedicated to my family, the best anyone could ask for, and in memory of Constance Harris

Chelsea House Publishers

Editor-in-Chief	Sally Cheney
Production Manager	Pamela Loos
Art Director	Sara Davis
Director of Production	Kim Shinners

The Chelsea House World Wide Web address is
http://www.chelseahouse.com

First Printing
1 3 5 7 9 8 6 4 2

**Produced by Pre-Press Company, Inc.,
East Bridgewater, MA 02333**

Bruce & Becky Durost Fish, 1974-
  Terry McMillan / by Bruce & Becky Durost Fish.
    96 pp.   cm. — (Black Americans of achievement)
  Includes bibliographical references and index.
Summary: A biography of the African American actor who rose to
the top of his profession, won an Academy Award, and was named
one of the most popular movie stars in 1998.
ISBN 0-7910-4692-3
      0-7910-4693-1 (pbk.)
1. McMillan, Terry, 1951-   —Juvenile literature. 2. Actors—
United States—Biography—Juvenile literature. 3. Afro-American
actors—Biography—Juvenile literature. [1. Washington, Denzel,
1954-   . 2. Actors and actresses. 3. Afro-Americans—Biography.]
I. Title. II. Series.
PN2287.W452H56 1998
791.43'028'092—dc21
[B]   98-15401
                                                    CIP
                                                    AC

Terry McMillan's latest book, A Day Late and a Dollar Short was published in January 2001. As an author she has reached a long-ignored market—educated black women like herself.

CONTENTS

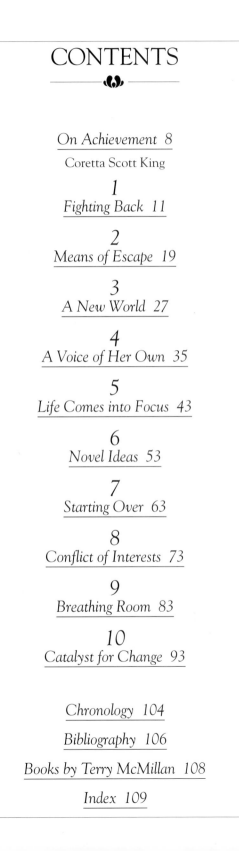

BLACK AMERICANS OF ACHIEVEMENT

HENRY AARON
baseball great

KAREEM ABDUL-JABBAR
basketball great

MUHAMMAD ALI
heavyweight champion

RICHARD ALLEN
religious leader and social activist

MAYA ANGELOU
author

LOUIS ARMSTRONG
musician

ARTHUR ASHE
tennis great

JOSEPHINE BAKER
entertainer

JAMES BALDWIN
author

TYRA BANKS
model

BENJAMIN BANNEKER
scientist and mathematician

COUNT BASIE
bandleader and composer

ANGELA BASSETT
actress

ROMARE BEARDEN
artist

HALLE BERRY
actress

MARY MCLEOD BETHUNE
educator

GEORGE WASHINGTON
CARVER
botanist

JOHNNIE COCHRAN
lawyer

SEAN "PUFFY" COMBS
music producer

BILL COSBY
entertainer

MILES DAVIS
musician

FREDERICK DOUGLASS
abolitionist editor

CHARLES DREW
physician

W. E. B. DU BOIS
scholar and activist

PAUL LAURENCE DUNBAR
poet

DUKE ELLINGTON
bandleader and composer

RALPH ELLISON
author

JULIUS ERVING
basketball great

LOUIS FARRAKHAN
political activist

ELLA FITZGERALD
singer

ARETHA FRANKLIN
entertainer

MORGAN FREEMAN
actor

MARCUS GARVEY
black nationalist leader

JOSH GIBSON
baseball great

WHOOPI GOLDBERG
entertainer

CUBA GOODING JR.
actor

ALEX HALEY
author

PRINCE HALL
social reformer

JIMI HENDRIX
musician

MATTHEW HENSON
explorer

GREGORY HINES
performer

BILLIE HOLIDAY
singer

LENA HORNE
entertainer

WHITNEY HOUSTON
singer and actress

LANGSTON HUGHES
poet

JANET JACKSON
musician

JESSE JACKSON
civil-rights leader and politician

MICHAEL JACKSON
entertainer

SAMUEL L. JACKSON
actor

T. D. JAKES
religious leader

JACK JOHNSON
heavyweight champion

MAGIC JOHNSON
basketball great

SCOTT JOPLIN
composer

BARBARA JORDAN
politician

MICHAEL JORDAN
basketball great

CORETTA SCOTT KING
civil-rights leader

MARTIN LUTHER KING, JR.
civil-rights leader

LEWIS LATIMER
scientist

SPIKE LEE
filmmaker

CARL LEWIS
champion athlete

JOE LOUIS
heavyweight champion

RONALD MCNAIR
astronaut

MALCOLM X
militant black leader

BOB MARLEY
musician

THURGOOD MARSHALL
Supreme Court justice

TERRY MCMILLAN
author

TONI MORRISON
author

ELIJAH MUHAMMAD
religious leader

EDDIE MURPHY
entertainer

JESSE OWENS
champion athlete

SATCHEL PAIGE
baseball great

CHARLIE PARKER
musician

ROSA PARKS
civil-rights leader

COLIN POWELL
military leader

PAUL ROBESON
singer and actor

JACKIE ROBINSON
baseball great

CHRIS ROCK
comedian and actor

DIANA ROSS
entertainer

WILL SMITH
actor

WESLEY SNIPES
actor

CLARENCE THOMAS
Supreme Court justice

SOJOURNER TRUTH
antislavery activist

HARRIET TUBMAN
antislavery activist

NAT TURNER
slave revolt leader

TINA TURNER
entertainer

ALICE WALKER
author

MADAM C. J. WALKER
entrepreneur

BOOKER T. WASHINGTON
educator

DENZEL WASHINGTON
actor

J. C. WATTS
politician

VANESSA WILLIAMS
singer and actress

OPRAH WINFREY
entertainer

TIGER WOODS
golf star

RICHARD WRIGHT
author

ON
ACHIEVEMENT

Coretta Scott King

Before you begin this book, I hope you will ask yourself what the word *excellence* means to you. I think it's a question we should all ask, and keep asking as we grow older and change. Because the truest answer to it should never change. When you think of excellence, perhaps you think of success at work; or of becoming wealthy; or meeting the right person, getting married, and having a good family life.

Those goals are worth striving for, but there is a better way to look at excellence. As Martin Luther King Jr. said in one of his last sermons, "I want you to be first in love. I want you to be first in moral excellence. I want you to be first in generosity. If you want to be important, wonderful. If you want to be great, wonderful. But recognize that he who is greatest among you shall be your servant."

My husband knew that the true meaning of achievement is service. When I met him, in 1952, he was already ordained as a Baptist minister and was working toward a doctoral degree at Boston University. I was studying at the New England Conservatory and dreamed of accomplishments in music. We married a year later, and after I graduated the following year we moved to Montgomery, Alabama. We didn't know it then, but our notions of achievement were about to undergo a dramatic change.

You may have read or heard about what happened next. What began with the boycott of a local bus line grew into a national crusade, and by the time he was assassinated in 1968 my husband had fashioned a black movement powerful enough to shatter forever the practice of racial segregation. What you may not have read about is where he learned to resist injustice without compromising his religious beliefs.

He adopted a strategy of nonviolence from a man of a different race, who lived in a different country and even practiced a different religion. The man was Mahatma Gandhi, the great leader of India, who devoted his life to serving humanity in the spirit of love and nonviolence. It was in these principles that Martin discovered his method for social reform. More than anything else, those two principles were the key to his achievements.

These books are about African Americans who served society through the excellence of their achievements. They form part of the rich history of black men and women in America—a history of stunning accomplishments in every field of human endeavor, from literature and art to science, industry, education, diplomacy, athletics, jurisprudence, even polar exploration.

Not all of the people in this history had the same ideals, but I think you will find that all of them had something in common. Like Martin Luther King Jr., they all decided to become "drum majors" and serve humanity. In that principle—whether it was expressed in books, inventions, or song— they found a goal and a guide outside themselves that showed them a way to serve others instead of living only for themselves.

Reading the stories of these courageous men and women not only helps us discover the principles that we will use to guide our own lives; it also teaches us about our black heritage and about America itself. It is crucial for us to know the heroes and heroines of our history and to realize that the price we paid in our struggle for equality in America was dear. But we must also understand that we have gotten as far as we have partly because America's democratic system and ideals made it possible.

We are still struggling with racism and prejudice. But the great men and women in this series are a tribute to the spirit of the country in which they have flourished. And that makes their stories special and worth knowing.

1

FIGHTING BACK

❧

TEENAGER TERRY MCMILLAN was never one to accept passively the status quo. She refused to allow her stepfather to continue beating and abusing her mother. If her mother would not defend herself, then Terry was determined to do whatever was necessary to end the violence in their home. Without thinking, Terry lifted her stepfather by the shirt and threw him. "The knife fell from his hand, and I grabbed it," she recalled in an interview with reporter Michael Shelden in the *Electronic Telegraph*. "I took that knife, and I pushed that point into his neck and said: 'Now, how does that feel?'"

Taking direct action in such a situation was in many ways a reaction to what Terry saw around her in her hometown of Port Huron, Michigan. Located on the shores of Lake Huron and the head of the St. Clair River, Port Huron is one of the few natural deepwater ports along the Great Lakes. The town was the boyhood home of inventor Thomas Alva Edison and was originally a lumber and shipbuilding center.

But by the time Terry's mother, Madeline Washington, discovered she was pregnant in 1951, Port Huron had become a railway center and was known for factories that produced machinery, tools, and auto parts. These factories thrived because they were located only about 60 miles

Terry McMillan grew up in Port Huron, Michigan, an industrial town near Detroit. Her childhood there taught her that she did not want anyone else to determine her destiny.

In the 1950s and 1960s, most of the adults in Terry's South Park neighborhood worked in local factories or commuted to Detroit to work in the Motor City's auto plants.

northeast of Detroit, and in the 1950s, the American automobile industry was booming.

Positioned across the river from Ontario, Canada, Port Huron had been an important stop in the Underground Railroad when slaves fled the South to seek freedom in Canada before the Civil War. Freedom, however, was no longer an issue among the black community of Port Huron. African-American families were simply trying to survive.

And most juniors in high school who found themselves pregnant felt they had few options except to marry the father of their unborn baby. That's exactly what Madeline Washington did. On June 9, 1951, she married 21-year-old Edward Lewis McMillan. Four and a half months later, on October 18, their first child, Terry Lynn, was born.

Young Terry's family moved frequently, but they always stayed within the South Park neighborhood, an area about 7 blocks wide and 10 blocks long, located well south of downtown Port Huron. South Park was predominantly black, and most of its residents found work in the local factories or by carpooling to Detroit, Mount Clemens, or New Haven. It took one and a half hours to reach Detroit by car, and slightly less time to reach the other two towns.

"Dirty, dirty, dirty," is how one woman who worked in a Chrysler supplier plant in New Haven described the work. "[B]ut I made money!"

Although Port Huron wasn't filled with the "Whites Only" signs found in the South, like many places in the North, unwritten rules segregated blacks and whites. Downtown Port Huron contained businesses for the largely white population that lived north of South Park. The only time black people were seen in many neighborhoods was when they were arriving or leaving the homes of wealthy white families where they worked as maids or cooks. A few blacks were able to get jobs as elevator inspectors in local banks, and a small number held positions in retail stores, but in reality African Americans in Port Huron had few employment opportunities outside of the factories.

Terry Lynn McMillan did not remain an only child for long. A little over a year after Terry was

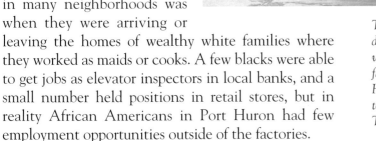

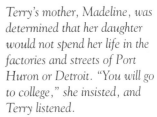

Terry's mother, Madeline, was determined that her daughter would not spend her life in the factories and streets of Port Huron or Detroit. "You will go to college," she insisted, and Terry listened.

born, she was joined by her brother Edwin. Within the next three years, Rosalyn, Crystal, and Vicki were born. The five young children created understandable chaos in the McMillan's home life, but Madeline and "Crook" (as Terry's father was called) added to the instability. Crook McMillan had two serious illnesses: diabetes and alcoholism. Drinking aggravated his diabetes, so Crook, a sanitation worker, often missed work. When this happened, he would get extremely frustrated and beat his wife. Terry has described how her mother would fight back and how the five children "would jump on him to break it up."

Despite being treated so poorly, Madeline McMillan was not willing to give up on her marriage. Although Terry wished her mother would do a better job of defending herself, she respected her mother's strength. "She was smart, bossy, aggressive—a no-nonsense woman," Terry recalled in a 1997 interview with Pam Janis. "She knew what it took to get things done and made sure we knew, too. She had five kids by the time she was 23—that can make or break you. It made her."

To supplement Crook's unreliable income, Madeline got jobs wherever she could, working in factories or cleaning people's homes. When she couldn't find work, she went on welfare. Not able to complete high school herself, Madeline was determined that her children would get a good education. From the time Terry began attending kindergarten at Cleveland Elementary School in South Park, she knew she was expected to do her best. Her first teacher, Mary Goschnik, remembers Terry as a very bright, happy child. "I would call Terry an A-minus student. She was always there, almost never absent. She had an outgoing personality. She was a happy person. All the kids around the neighborhood were friends."

As the oldest McMillan child, Terry took on the responsibility of caring for her younger brother and

sisters while her parents worked—cooking their meals, washing their hair, and making sure that they did their homework. Money was always tight. During some cold Michigan winters, the McMillan home went without a phone, heat, or electricity, but they always managed to have food on the table for their growing family. "There were a couple winter nights I remember my teeth chattering," Terry has reported, "But I don't remember ever feeling poor. I hate that word."

The physical condition of Terry's father continued to deteriorate, and he would be absent for days at a time, often drinking himself into oblivion. At those times when the family was together, the conflicts between Madeline and Crook increased, and the five children saw repeated instances of domestic violence.

"It was almost like it was entertainment for them on Friday nights even though sometimes it got scary," Terry recalled in an interview with *Ebony*. "I hated the fear of worrying if one day they were going to kill

Although Michigan winters were often hard for the McMillan family, Terry would later say, "I don't remember ever feeling poor. I hate that word."

each other. And I knew that when I grew up, if a man couldn't deal with his anger any other way, he wasn't going to take it out on me."

In May 1963, Terry's parents finally divorced. Madeline charged her husband with "extreme and repeated cruelties" and was given custody of the five children.

With the departure of her father, 11-year-old Terry felt even more responsibility for her family. Although 1963 marked the assassination of President John F. Kennedy and nearby Detroit was a center of activity in the civil rights movement, Port Huron remained relatively unaffected by these national events. Like Terry, most of the residents of South Park were much more concerned about their personal problems.

Terry, now in junior high school, was always encouraged by her mother to value her education. "You will go to college," Terry's mother told her repeatedly. "And you're not going with a baby." Madeline was determined that her eldest daughter was not going to end up as she had: unmarried and pregnant. She did not need to argue about this with Terry, who resolutely applied herself to her schoolwork.

Home life for Terry and her siblings soon began to include her mother's new boyfriend, Alvin "Nicky" Tillman. Thirteen years younger than Terry's mother, and only about five years older than Terry herself, Nicky had been born in Mississippi and worked as a laborer. Unlike Terry's father, Tillman managed to hold jobs. This quality probably appealed to Madeline, who had spent most of her adult life bearing the total responsibility for herself and her five children.

But Nicky Tillman also had the tendency to become violent. And it was during one of those moments that Terry held a knife to his throat.

In interviews, Terry recalls the event: "I told him, 'You know what? You touch my mother again, and I will slit your throat.' And he knew—he knew—that if he said the wrong thing, I would slit his throat. And I would have."

Before she completed junior high school, Terry had developed a reputation in her family as a fire-brand. She refused to tolerate either abuse or passivity. And she knew that she didn't want anyone else determining her destiny, even though as yet she had no idea what her destiny would be. That was about to change.

2

MEANS OF ESCAPE

❦

URING TERRY MCMILLAN'S sophomore year at Port Huron High School, she took a job as a student page at the St. Clair County Public Library in downtown Port Huron. Paid only $1.25 an hour, she was, like her brother and sisters doing everything she could to help her single mother support the family. "At fifteen years old, all I was concerned about was what I was going to do with that thirty-two dollars I was getting as my paycheck," she said. "I had no fantasies about being a writer."

Terry's job at the library, however, did much more than add to the family's income. Until she started working as a student page, the only books she had read were those on the required reading list at school. There were no books at home other than the family Bible, and she had never been read to by either her mother or father.

As was typical in most American schools during the 1960s, at Port Huron the books assigned to students were written by white writers, mostly men. Terry thus had dutifully read works by Ralph Waldo Emerson, William Faulkner, Nathaniel Hawthorne, Ernest Hemingway, Thomas Mann, and Henry David Thoreau, but she thought their books were boring. She also assumed that all writers were white. "I didn't know about any black writers when I was fifteen—none," she would later explain.

By the mid-1960s events in nearby Detroit—from the growth of the Motown music scene to the race riots of 1967—were making Terry aware of a world beyond Port Huron.

Terry McMillan's job at the public library introduced her to new authors and contributed to her success as a writer. She particularly identified with Louisa May Alcott who, although white, was poor and a woman who had helped to support her family, much like Terry.

But the library changed her view of reading. For the first time, Terry read books that she chose to read because they looked interesting. Reading became exciting. Books in the travel section made her fantasize about life in other countries and at other times—life that was much different from her experiences in Port Huron. She also stumbled upon a biography of 19th-century American female writer Louisa May Alcott, the author of *Little Women*. As Terry read about Louisa's childhood, she was stunned by the similarities with her own life. As a young girl, Louisa had helped to support her family. She described living on bread, water, fruit, and vegetables for days on end. She wrote about her large family being crammed into a ramshackle old farmhouse near the Boston docks.

The biography was a revelation to Terry. "I was excited because I had not really read about poor white folks before," she later explained. For the first time, Terry McMillan had discovered a kindred spirit through reading.

Similarities also existed between Alcott's Boston and McMillan's Port Huron. Not only were their two hometowns built beside bodies of water, but both places were made up of striking contrasts between the rich and the poor. Louisa described her first experience walking outside her poor neighborhood and seeing the opulent homes of the wealthy. While working at the library, Terry like Alcott was taken by the paved streets and clean, bright homes fronted by sidewalks—a stark contrast to the rundown wooden

Discovering black authors' writings, including work by James Baldwin (above), was an unexpected benefit to teenage library worker Terry McMillan.

homes in South Park, where most of the streets were unpaved.

Terry soon discovered other writers while working at the library. One day as she was shelving books, she happened to glance at the photograph on the back cover of a book. She could hardly believe her eyes. Staring back at her was the face of a black man. "Almost every book I used to put up was by a white author," she explained. "So it never dawned on me that black people wrote books."

The author she discovered was James Baldwin, the renowned African-American writer and civil-rights activist. By the mid-1960s his published works included *Go Tell It on the Mountain*, *The Amen Corner*, *Notes of a Native Son*, *Giovanni's Room*, *Nobody Knows My Name*, *Another Country*,

The Fire Next Time, Blues for Mister Charlie, and *Going to Meet the Man.* Even after that encounter, Terry had no idea that the books of black men actually had anything of interest or relevance for her or that the books also contained bitter indictments of how whites treated blacks in America. Thus, although captivated by the idea of a black writer, Terry still did not read his books. "I was too afraid," she later said in a *Washington Post* article. "I couldn't imagine that he'd have anything better or different to say than Thomas Mann, Henry Thoreau, Ralph Waldo Emerson. . . . Needless to say, I was not just naive, but had not yet acquired an ounce of black pride."

In spite of her limited exposure to her African-American heritage and culture, national events that could no longer be ignored, even in Port Huron, were beginning to make Terry aware of issues beyond her own family's survival. Racial riots broke out in nearby Detroit during the summer of 1967, leaving 43 people dead. Then in 1968, Rev. Martin Luther King Jr. was assassinated, as was Senator Robert F. Kennedy just hours after winning the Democratic presidential primary in California.

Changes were also taking place in the McMillan household. On October 8, 1967, just 10 days before Terry's 16th birthday and only a few weeks into her junior year of high school, her mother married Nicky Tillman. Once again, Madeline McMillan Tillman thought she could change a violent man. Once again, she was wrong. The fact that they were married did not change Nicky's behavior. A little more than a year later, on November 18, 1968, Nicky left. It isn't known whether he chose to move out or whether Madeline threw him out.

Using the same attorney she had used before, Terry's mother filed for divorce. On January 17, 1969, a restraining order was served on Tillman based on Madeline Tillman's petition that the "defendant has struck and hit the plaintiff, and has broken windows in the home of the plaintiff, and the plaintiff is apprehensive for her own safety and the well-being of her children."

Three days later, Nicky Tillman received a summons for divorce. The complaint alleged that "during the marriage defendant has been guilty of acts of extreme and repeated cruelties." The divorce was finalized on March 17, 1969. That same year, Edward "Crook" McMillan died of complications from his diabetes and alcoholism. The five McMillan children were once again living with a single mother, but in many ways, life was much more stable than it had been in years.

Terry, however, had seen enough of poverty and was determined to find a way out. "The basement of our house was always flooded and I remember we used to have to get in this little boat my brother had gotten for Christmas and paddle over to the washer and dryer to get the clothes in and out," she recalled in an interview with *Ebony*. "And cross your fingers that you didn't drop any of them in that nasty water on the way back. . . . When I went to high school, I told my mother, 'When I graduate, I'm outta here 'cause this is not the real world.'"

During her high school years, Terry did manage to do more than work and study. She also enjoyed parties and sleepovers with her two best friends, Cynthia Morgan and Bernadine Harvey. The threesome were inseparable, going to ball games, the rec center, and dances together. Sometimes they saw live bands perform. Other times they danced to Motown hits from James Brown, Diana Ross and the Supremes, and Aretha Franklin, or they listened to the jazz tunes of Miles Davis and John Coltrane.

Black and white race relations turned confrontational in late 1960s America, sometimes erupting into rioting and arson. On July 24, 1967, the second day of rioting, Michigan State Police helped patrol Detroit.

Some of Terry's neighbors thought her younger sisters were good looking and that Terry was something of an ugly duckling. And she was perceived as more assertive, more determined to reach out and take what she wanted from life. As the spring of 1969 came to a close, Terry was getting ready to take her high school diploma and get on with making her life into whatever she wanted.

During her years in high school, Terry was not exposed to her heritage as a black woman. The school simply did not offer much that could help her broaden her perspective. When Terry graduated, the high school was celebrating its centennial but the Afro-American club of Port Huron High had just been founded. Its purpose was "to seek a better understanding of Negro history and literature." In 1969, African-American studies programs in colleges and universities had just begun to develop and very few high schools offered any courses on the subject.

Black students also had few role models to follow in their schools. In Terry's yearbook, only two of the teachers pictured were African Americans and only 3 of the 33 student council members were black.

An interesting photo in that 1969 yearbook showed the business education department's office-practice class. Included in the photo was Terry McMillan, a star typist throughout her high school years. Along with her ability to take shorthand, typing was the skill she would need to launch herself into the next stage of her life.

Terry still wasn't sure what she wanted to become, but she was determined to get out of Port Huron and thus avoid having to work in a factory or become a domestic servant. She knew she couldn't sing or play an instrument, which ruled out heading for Detroit and trying for a contract at Motown Records. She only sensed that she needed a different environment, a place that held more diversity than

Port Huron. "I think the fact that my father died so young [at 39 years old] had a lot to do with my attitude," Terry has said about her decision to leave Michigan. "I knew things could be snatched away; that you might not get a second chance."

Whatever the reasons, at some point between her June graduation and October, she left Port Huron, and by the fall of 1969, she was living in Los Angeles. Although she could not have known it at the time, the decision to move to California would totally change the direction of her life.

3
A NEW WORLD

⟪⟫

To 17-YEAR-OLD Terry McMillan, California was a new world, a world she could not even have imagined in Port Huron, Michigan. The palm trees, the high ridges and mountains, the warm winters were like a dream. And while the people of Port Huron were mostly African American or white, Los Angeles was a melting pot, a place where all ethnic backgrounds could be found.

Terry's first step when she reached L.A. was to get a job working as a keypunch operator. She gradually became established in her new city, managed to save $300 in her first year, and was soon joined by her mother and younger siblings. During that year, Terry came across a catalog for Los Angeles City College, a community college. She was struck by a class called "Afro-American Literature." She knew that tuition at the college was free for students who had lived in Los Angeles for at least one year, so after she had satisfied that requirement, she enrolled at the college and began her formal education in black culture and history.

Terry came to the class thinking that there would not be enough black writers to fill an entire college course, but she soon learned differently, discovering Countee Cullen, Ralph Ellison, Langston Hughes, Zora Neale Hurston, and Richard Wright, among

Los Angeles was for Terry, like many before her, a chance for a new and better life. Moving there and enrolling in Los Angeles City College would be the first step on the road to a career as a writer.

others. "I accumulated and gained a totally new insight about, and perception of, our lives as black people, as if I had been an outsider and was finally let in," she later wrote about that period of her life. "To discover that our lives held as much significance and importance as our white counterparts was more than gratifying, it was exhilarating."

In a later interview with *Ebony,* she recalled, "It was an incredible awakening. I realized there was a whole world out here that I had no idea existed."

At about the same time, Terry fell in love. Having escaped Port Huron, discovered a new world of African-American literature, and developed a secure relationship, Terry was on top of the world. But that all changed in 1971 when her boyfriend broke up with her. Twenty-year-old Terry was devastated. For the first time, she turned to writing to express her feelings.

"I did not sit down and say, 'I'm going to write a poem about this,'" she later explained. "It was more like magic. I didn't even know I was writing a poem until I had written it. Afterward, I felt lighter, as if something had happened to lessen the pain."

A friend of hers saw the poem. He had just started a black literary magazine at Los Angeles City College. To Terry's amazement, he not only liked the poem, he asked if he could publish it. With that small encouragement, Terry began writing more poems.

"I started writing more poetry after that, because it seemed like it was gratifying," Terry said in an interview for *1999 Writer's Yearbook.* "It felt good to be able to express how you felt and it was a way to react to things, and you could keep it to yourself. That's how it started, and it just kind of evolved." Many of her early poems began to be published in college publications. They touched on a number of topics but were primarily reflections of a young black woman finding her place in the world.

In spite of the popularity of her poetry, Terry was not interested in becoming a professional writer. Life in Port Huron had taught her the value of a steady income, and she knew that most writers—particularly poets—could not make a living from the sales of their work. She had no intention of choosing a profession that would leave her in poverty, having to relive the hardships of her childhood. She also had her doubts about just how good her writing was. "I made the mistake of writing a poem

Through her courses at college Terry learned that she should be proud of her race. Books by authors like Alex Haley (above) helped bring about this change.

in college and was encouraged to take a writing class," she recounted at *The Detroit News* Spring Book & Author Luncheon in May 1997. "I was told I had talent. I didn't believe it."

Having seen firsthand how poverty, substance abuse, and discrimination could destroy people's lives, she decided to become a social worker so that she could help other people and make some difference in their lives. She immediately started taking courses to reach that goal.

In spite of her pragmatic approach to career choice, Terry could not turn her back on her love of literature. While at the community college, she immersed herself in the writings of African-American writers such as James Baldwin, Gwendolyn Brooks, Toni Morrison, and Alice Walker. Reading *The Autobiography of Malcolm X*, which Malcolm X had dictated to Alex Haley, revolutionized Terry's attitude toward being black. She suddenly understood more about black history and culture and realized that she should be proud of being a member of her race.

After completing two years at the community college, Terry transferred to the University of California at Berkeley, more than 400 miles north of Los Angeles and across the bay from San Francisco. During the 1960s, Berkeley had become synonymous with student protests and sit-ins. In a famous incident during 1969, the National Guard had been called in to control a student demonstration in People's Park.

The chancellor of the university at that time, Roger W. Heyns, responded to students' concerns, but he also did not lose sight of the university's future. He completed several building projects, such as a new science building and an art museum. He also began a special minority admissions program, and that program helped Terry McMillan earn her degree.

By the time she arrived in Berkeley, Terry knew her heart wasn't in sociology and she didn't think she

could fulfill all the course requirements for that major. Realizing that writing came more easily to her, she switched her major to journalism.

But school meant more to Terry than simply attending classes, completing assignments, and working to keep food on the table. She quickly developed a circle of friends. They watched movies together, threw parties, and visited the local beaches and the surrounding mountains.

Terry transferred to UC-Berkeley (above) after two years at Los Angeles Community College and switched her major from sociology to journalism.

In 1969, students at the University of California at Berkeley protest near popular People's Park. America in the late 1960s was rife with political and cultural tensions, especially on college campuses. American military involvement in Vietnam was a major source of these tensions.

On the politically aware Berkeley campus, Terry couldn't avoid hearing about the controversy surrounding the Vietnam War. In 1971, the Twenty-sixth Amendment to the Constitution had been ratified, lowering the voting age from 21 to 18. That meant that almost every student on campus qualified to vote. To many students, the 1972 election had been a referendum on whether or not America should be fighting in Vietnam.

Students at Berkeley watched the reelection of Richard Nixon, the signing in Paris of a peace treaty giving North Vietnam control of all Vietnam, and the resignation of Vice President Spiro T. Agnew. The Watergate hearings began, and in the summer of 1974, Richard Nixon resigned from office rather than face certain impeachment and a Senate trial that he was sure to lose.

These events fueled discussions in journalism schools across the nation. Most journalism school students yearned to become the next Bob Woodward or Carl Bernstein, the *Washington Post* reporters who

Although most of Terry's fellow students in the School of Journalism at UC-Berkeley wanted to follow in the footsteps of reporters like the Washington Post's *Bob Woodward and Carl Bernstein (right), Terry knew she needed a less restricting outlet for her creativity.*

had first reported on the White House cover-up of the Watergate break-in. Investigative reporting became a popular career choice.

Terry felt differently. While she continued to major in journalism, she knew the field wasn't a perfect fit for her. The highly structured "who, what, when, where, and why" format of news stories went against her spontaneous, creative bent. She was much more comfortable creating stories based on her personal experiences and finding a creative outlet for the emotions and questions she faced.

During the 1974–75 school year, Terry enrolled in "Introduction to Fiction." The class wasn't required, but she was drawn to it. And as she was to find out, taking a course from 36-year-old Ishmael Reed would have long-reaching effects on the rest of her life.

4

A VOICE OF HER OWN

❧

ISHMAEL REED WAS a poet, novelist, and essayist who was part African American and part Cherokee. He also was committed to developing writers and to expanding people's understanding of American literature so that it would include writers from diverse ethnic backgrounds. As he got to know the students that year in his introduction to fiction class, he was impressed by their abilities.

"Out of that class came four other novelists: Mona Simpson, Fae Ng, Katie Trueblood, and Mitch Berman," he recalled. "I never had a class like that before, where that amount of talent came out of one class. That was a very lively class—they challenged each other."

Terry's natural writing style marked her as unusual. "I did not interfere with Terry's style," Reed explained. "I think it was fully formed. She had something to say. . . . She's not illustrating some kind of ideology, she's writing about people."

So how did he help develop Terry's writing? "Most good writers have all the stuff in their head, they just have to structure it," he says. "So I helped her on form. What to leave out and what to leave in. That's a basic problem for most beginning writers. She became a cleaner writer in the workshop. . . . What separated her from a lot of other people was her drive. She was focused about that."

Even as a student-writer Terry had a voice of her own. She didn't try to write like the authors she admired, a mistake that young writers sometimes make.

35

A journalist of the 1920s, Ring Lardner's style of writing in a distinctive yet unpretentious voice appealed to Terry McMillan's desire to describe characters and scenes as she saw them. Lardner began his career reporting sports but later focused on humor and satire.

Terry, herself, saw things somewhat differently. "I don't even know what made me take my first fiction writing class, but I had heard of Ishmael Reed," she said in an interview with Anne Bowling. "I ended up writing a story for his class, and he said my voice was just amazing. I didn't know what he was talking about. I have a deep voice, so when I talk, a lot of times people think I'm a guy. Until he explained what 'voice' meant, I didn't even know what he was talking about."

What her teacher had noticed was that Terry had a unique way of expressing herself. She wasn't trying to write like some famous author or with language that didn't come naturally to her. Terry's writing sounded like Terry and could be easily identified. She had her own style.

Terry continued immersing herself in the works of good writers. One of her favorites became Ring Lardner, a satiric journalist. "As soon as I read Ring Lardner," she later said, "his voice jumped off the page. What he was writing about was tragic, and I was cracking up. I realized that it was the same sort of thing I was trying to do in my stuff. Ring Lardner said, 'It's OK, Terry, to write the way that you talk.' Ring Lardner was the one who freed me up."

She also admired the work of Langston Hughes, a Harlem Renaissance poet and writer. Among other things, Hughes wrote about his traveling adventures, and Terry had been drawn to books about travel since her days shelving books in the

Fellow UC-Berkeley classmate and published author Mona Simpson sharpened her and Terry McMillan's competitive creative spirit as students in Reed's class.

Port Huron library. Ann Petry was another writer who attracted Terry's attention. She particularly liked Petry's novel *The Street*, about a black woman raising her son in the violence and poverty of Harlem in the 1940s.

After completing her fiction class, Terry continued to write. "Writing became an outlet for my dissatisfactions, distaste, and my way of trying to make sense of what was happening around me," she said. "It was my way of trying to fix what I thought was broken. It later became the only way to explore personally what I didn't understand."

As she wrote, she expanded beyond poetry to creating short stories. Her first, "The End," was set in Detroit's lower east side. Drawing from her

UC-Berkeley professor and award-winning writer Ishmael Reed remains a friend and mentor to Terry McMillan. Reed, winner of a 1998 MacArthur Fellowship Award, helped Terry learn to edit her own work.

childhood knowledge of work at the Ford factory, the story featured a young black man, Pobre Blackstone, who worked on the assembly line and dreamed about the world coming to an end. "The End" so impressed Ishmael Reed that he published it in the 1976 edition of his literary magazine, *Yardbird Reader.* "We were devoted to publishing multicultural writers," he explained. "I realized that students could write as well as anybody else, so I began to include students."

Another short story she wrote during her years at Berkeley was an attempt to explore how her own mother had been able to raise five children under such difficult circumstances. The untitled story was set in the fictional town of Point Haven and featured a black mother, Mildred Peacock. "I wanted to show a middle-aged woman—black and for the most part deprived—who focused on raising her kids without really devoting any time to her life and her future," Terry explained. "I wanted to show that in getting from Point One to Point Ten, she did enjoy making love, that she did know how to have a good time, and that she didn't sit around and cry and whine."

As the number of Terry's short stories grew, she thought she might be able to get some of them published, maybe as a collection of short stories. Although she managed to get individual stories published in magazines like *Yardbird Reader*, she wasn't able to find a book publisher who was interested in her writing. This mixed success only reinforced her feelings that writing was no way to try to make a living.

Just because she didn't plan a career as a writer didn't mean Terry wasn't interested in learning about writing and ideas. She struck up conversations with professors, even if she didn't take classes from them. One such teacher was Clyde Taylor, at that time a professor of African-American Studies. "With professors, most students have a formal attitude: I'll see him in his office," Taylor observed. "Terry would just start a conversation, friend to friend. . . . She did seem to be searching. She asked for advice: 'What do you think about this or that?'"

Although Terry was not afraid to talk to anybody, she was much less assertive about her writing abilities. "Although she had a way of being direct—she would come up and ask you any kind of question—about her literary talent she was quiet," Clyde Taylor said. "She didn't seem to push [reading her poetry] hard—if someone asked her to she would. She was molding herself, and the Bay Area was a great environment for that in those days. Literary people would encourage each other. There was a Third World consciousness, the beginnings of feminism, and youth, plus the remainders of a counterculture."

Professor Taylor also observed that Terry associated with a wide variety of people. "The circles she moved in were not strictly black or female," he said. "Terry is a poetic personality. I think that's where that creative thing comes from. But I suspect that she comes from a background where nobody expected anything from anybody."

In the spring of 1976, Terry McMillan graduated from Berkeley with a bachelor's degree in journalism, but she still didn't know what she wanted to do with her life. She worked in an affluent suburb of San Francisco as a typist while she considered her options. By January 1978, Terry was living in San Anselmo, a small town about 20 miles north of San Francisco. She questioned friends and family about what she should do next. She still loved writing, but she also refused to believe that she could support herself through her writing. She knew too many writers, and she had heard too many horror stories about writers not getting paid or working multiple jobs to keep a roof over their heads.

That month, she wrote a lengthy letter to Ishmael Reed, who had remained a friend and mentor to her after she graduated from Berkeley. She described how unlikely it was for her to earn her living by becoming a poet or playwright, and certainly not by being a novelist because she'd never written anything longer than 15 pages. But she understood how important it was to her to express herself to others. She'd decided to go to film school, she told him. She saw films as an avenue that would give her the self-expression she craved and still provide a decent living. At the close of the letter, Terry asked Reed if he'd write a letter of recommendation for her.

With his assistance, Terry was accepted at Columbia University Film School in New York City. She enrolled in the master's degree of fine arts program and planned on studying screenwriting. Soon 26-year-old Terry was packing her belongings and heading for the East Coast.

5

LIFE COMES INTO FOCUS

T ERRY MCMILLAN ARRIVED at Columbia University in 1979. The campus was located in the Morningside Heights area of uptown New York. Apartments on nearby Riverside Drive were selling for several hundred thousand dollars, while many people living in Harlem, just east of Morningside Park, faced terrible poverty. Racial tensions were never far from the surface.

Students enrolled in the School of Fine Arts spent their first year taking core courses in the master of fine arts curriculum. These classes introduced them to writing, directing, and the team effort required in putting a film together. Along with those required courses, Terry and her classmates chose various elective courses. At the end of the year, each student, with the input of a faculty advisor, declared an area of concentration such as directing or producing. Terry chose to concentrate in screenwriting.

The second year of the program required students to work intensively in their area of concentration. Screenwriting majors were required to write a feature-length script. Once that was completed, they began work on a thesis project, usually a feature-length screenplay. The thesis project was designed to demonstrate that the student had original ideas and had mastered the basic techniques of

Terry headed East, to graduate school at New York City's Columbia University. She chose to study filmmaking, a visual expression of the written word.

dialogue, characterization, and cinematic and dramatic structure.

Terry, however, did not complete the program. In later interviews, she explained that she found the school to be "very racist" and that she and an African student—the only blacks in the class—were not being treated right. She decided to withdraw from the program, but she was not going to abandon her writing.

To support herself, Terry registered with an employment agency and worked as a word processor in law firms. The true focus of her energies was on fine-tuning her short stories, but her writing activities had to be wedged in between the time demands of working for prestigious New York City law firms. Often, she was required to work late into the night. The work did pay quite well, however, which was a good thing since living in New York City was expensive, and everyone who worked in a law firm was expected to dress well. Terry liked the nice clothes, and she gained another valuable education at the various law firms she worked for.

By inputting the wide variety of letters sent by attorneys, Terry learned the language of letter writing and all the different things a letter could accomplish: clarifying situations; explaining consequences if action were not taken; requesting information or action. Terry was so popular at the law firms where she worked that they often requested her by name.

Columbia University features Italian Renaissance style buildings designed at the beginning of the 20th century by the famous architectural firm McKim, Mead & White. Founded in 1754, Columbia has been supported by some of America's wealthiest citizens. Its current location is surrounded by an eclectic mix of neighborhoods, representing people from an amazing variety of ethnic and economic backgrounds. Walking down the streets, one typically hears other people speaking English, Yiddish, Spanish, and a variety of Asian and Eastern European languages.

Columbia is within walking distance of the Cathedral of St. John the Divine, which is the world's largest Gothic-style cathedral; Grant's tomb, a national historic site where the 18th president is buried; and Riverside Park, located on a more-than-two-mile stretch along the banks of the Hudson River. Both Riverside Park, to the west of the university, and Morningside Park, to the east of the university, were designed by the noted 19th-century landscape architect Frederick Law Olmstead.

One of the law firms at which Terry worked was Barovick Lonecky Braun Schwartz & Kay, located at One Dag Hammarskjold Plaza within walking distance of the United Nations. This firm was a powerhouse in the world of entertainment; among their clients were the Beach Boys, Casablanca Records, Neil Diamond, Bob Dylan, George Harrison, Steely Dan, and Donna Summer. At Barovick, Terry would learn to read movie contracts, which would serve her well later.

During this time, Terry was also struggling with a habit that threatened to destroy her life. While in college, she had begun snorting cocaine and drinking. "I would say this is so *stupid*," she recalled in an interview with *Ebony*. "Here I am graduating from one of the most prestigious universities in the country and I'm sitting here snorting this powder up my nose. I used to mess up everybody's high because I'd be sitting there drinking my tequila shots, saying, 'One day I'm not even going to be doing this.' And they'd [her friends] say, 'Terry, *please*. Will you just be quiet and pass the mirror.'"

This behavior continued after she left Columbia. On mornings when Terry got called into work after a wild night, she'd claim she had an emergency, such as broken plumbing. The time she'd be given to deal with her "emergency" would allow her to sober up enough to be able to work. She rationalized her behavior by noting that some of her coworkers were obviously no strangers to hangovers themselves. But a series of events made her decide it was time to quit.

The first happened when she was shopping in an antique store and found herself comparing the cost of the furniture to how much cocaine the same amount of money would buy. "I said this dresser is two-and-a-half grams. I could have had that," she recounted. "And as I walked around the store, I started thinking I had snorted up a whole roomful of furniture."

Shortly after that, she looked in a mirror and saw her father's face. It reminded her of his early death and the pain he had put his family through because of his alcohol addiction. Then in the early morning hours of her 30th birthday, she was lying in bed drinking vodka, trying to come down from her cocaine high. "I said, 'You know what, Terry? You're thirty years old and this is enough,'" she recalled in an interview. "I had to be at work in a few hours and I had about a half gram left. So I said, 'I'll go ahead and do this and get through the day. And that's it.' I haven't touched it since."

But her drinking continued. One evening in the winter of 1983, Terry got what she calls "sloppy drunk" and locked her boyfriend out of the house. Then she passed out. "When I came to, he said, 'Terry, baby, I think you have a problem,'" she recounted. "And I said, 'You know what? I think I do, too.' The next morning, February 22, 1983, I went to an [Alcoholics Anonymous] meeting. I went for 90 days until I stopped."

By the spring of 1983, her system was clean of both alcohol and cocaine. In interviews throughout the succeeding years, she has always maintained that she has never used either substance after that time.

Terry continued to do well at the law firms. In 1983, she earned $15 an hour, averaging a salary of $750 a week. Sometimes she earned as much as $1,000 in a week. Because she didn't have family responsibilities, she frequently worked shifts that no one else was interested in taking. Often she would complete an assignment at one firm, only to go to another firm and work a few more hours that same day.

Terry no longer lived near Columbia University. She traveled into Manhattan from her brownstone apartment in the busy Fort Greene neighborhood of

Brooklyn. The tree-lined street was near the Brooklyn Academy of Music, Pratt Institute, and the Lafayette Avenue Presbyterian Church (where the Emancipation Proclamation is said to have been drafted).

A few doors down the street from Terry's place was another brownstone that had been converted into a rooming house. One of the people who lived there was Leonard Welch, a black construction worker who was about 30 years old and who used his carpentry skills on the side to make extra money. In 1982, he took on the job of installing wooden floors in Terry's brownstone. When Terry saw the muscular six-foot four-inch man laying floors in her building, she was smitten. Leonard had dropped out of high school in the 11th grade and earned his high school equivalency diploma. He worked out in a gym three times a week, and at the time Terry met him, he was separated from his wife and children.

Welch was equally attracted to Terry and soon after they first met he moved into her apartment. Their relationship was stormy. While Terry was outspoken and driven, working hard every week, Leonard was struggling to establish himself. Construction jobs were hard to come by, and Leonard's financial situation was anything but stable.

Unable to make a steady income and living with a woman who seemed to find work effortlessly, Leonard grew increasingly frustrated. He would take out his feelings on Terry. Verbal abuse escalated to the point where Leonard slapped her. But still Terry stuck with the relationship, hoping she could make it work out.

Between the pressures of work and her up-and-down relationship with Leonard, Terry still made time for writing. She typically got up at about 4:30 in the morning and wrote for four hours. This gave her complete quiet in which to work—no interruptions. Then while riding the subway to wherever she might be working that day, she'd mark changes on her rough draft with a red pen. Computers were rarely found outside the workplace, so during down time at the office, she would type her work into the computer and save it on a disk.

Terry was working particularly hard on the short story about Mildred Peacock which she had begun back at Berkeley. She named it "Mama," and decided she wanted to look seriously for a place to get it published. At that point, research became her weapon. She educated herself about writers and writing and pursued every lead for a place that might provide her with either time or money to write. She read *Writer's Digest*, *The Writer*, and *Coda* magazines to get ideas for markets as well as the names of writer's organizations, meetings, and conferences. She bought books about writers and writing, looking for anything that

would help her improve her work. She maintained contacts with writing friends she had made over the years, especially Ishmael Reed, her teacher back in Berkeley. And she tried to establish new contacts within the New York City writing community.

All of this research made Terry aware of artists' colonies—organizations that provided room and board for anywhere from one week to seven months so that artists and writers could take a leave of absence from daily responsibilities and focus their energies on a specific project. Some colonies were "quiet" colonies, where the emphasis was on solitude and silence. Others encouraged residents to perform their works and attend workshops as well as spend time on their projects. Interested candidates applied by filling out an application form and submitting samples of their work, which were then reviewed by a panel of experts. Those artists who were selected were invited to stay at the artists' colony.

Terry was particularly struck by information she received about Yaddo, an artists' colony located in Saratoga Springs, New York, about 200 miles north of New York City. A "quiet" colony, Yaddo had clear

While attending Saratoga Springs' Yaddo Writers' Colony in 1982 and 1983, Terry got uninterrupted time and space to devote to her writing.

Mystery writer Mary Higgins Clark is one of the many professional writers who, like Terry, stayed at the esteemed MacDowell colony.

rules mandating behavior: between 9 A.M. and 4 P.M., as well as any time after 10 P.M., were quiet hours when artists worked without interruption from fellow residents or guests. The residents ate breakfast and dinner together, but they each took a packed lunch to their studio to make it easier to work uninterrupted during the day. Winding trails through the surrounding woodland, tennis courts, a swimming pool, bicycles, and a Ping-Pong table provided the only entertainment.

To Terry, such an environment sounded like a wonderful change from the city. In 1982, she applied for a residency at Yaddo and was accepted. She spent two weeks there, savoring every moment. In 1983, she visited Yaddo again, as well as another artists' colony: the MacDowell Colony in Peterborough, New Hampshire. Past residents of MacDowell Colony have won more than 50 Pulitzer Prizes and 7 MacArthur Foundation Genius Awards. James Baldwin offered this comment about his experience there: "I will be very glad . . . to be working at the Colony—which for many years now has lived in my mind as a refuge and a workshop and the place in which I most wanted to be when the time comes, as it perpetually does, to crouch in order to spring."

Terry was excited to be accepted at such a prestigious colony and spent 44 days there during the spring of 1983. According to the 1983 MacDowell newsletter, the 49 artists who arrived for residencies during that spring included 23 writers. Terry was associating with writers such as Mary Higgins Clark, who was working on her fifth novel; Claude Brown, author of *Manchild in the Promised Land*; and Audre Lorde, who was completing a collection of essays.

The time Terry spent at Yaddo and MacDowell was quite productive. She had enlarged her short story into a book of more than 400 pages. But she knew it still needed work, and she kept looking for other avenues of improving her writing. One Sunday, she happened to watch the television program *Like It Is*, hosted by African-American journalist Gil Noble. His guests were the writers Maya Angelou and John Oliver Killens. During the program, Terry learned that both writers were members of the Harlem Writers Guild. She added that name to her list of organizations to check out.

Soon Terry was accepted as a member of the Harlem Writers Guild and was attending the weekly Monday evening meetings. She met established writers such as Rosa Guy, Grace Edwards, and Sarah Elizabeth Wright. Although Terry didn't realize it at the time, she had taken all the steps needed for the major changes that were about to take place in her life.

6

NOVEL IDEAS

T HE HARLEM WRITERS Guild helped Terry focus her fiction writing. She learned from more experienced writers and received the type of encouragement that she had found in few relationships up to that time. One evening, she read her short story "Mama."

"After I finished reading, the room got real quiet," she said later in an interview. "Finally somebody said, 'That doesn't sound like a short story to me. It sounds like the beginning of a novel. You sure can write!'"

Terry also found a good friend in Doris Jean Austin, a writer who, like her, had experienced a turbulent childhood. When she was 12 years old, Doris was raped by two neighbors who told her that no one would believe her if she ever told anyone what they had done. Although the men were eventually caught, young Doris couldn't stand the pressure of the stares and whispers she endured. She transferred to another school and eventually suppressed her memories of the rape.

Later as an adult, Doris went through a divorce, watched her mother die from cancer, and had cancer treatments herself. When she discovered that she would survive her cancer, Doris realized that she needed to go through counseling so that she could come to terms with the many devastating things

Terry McMillan says of her parting with Leonard Welch, "I had to really stop and think about my own well-being and the future of my son."

that had happened to her in such a short time. In undergoing her therapy, Doris remembered the rape. Writing became a tool to help her put herself back together. Both she and Terry McMillan were using fiction to help themselves understand the world around them.

Terry described her experiences with the Harlem Writers Guild this way: "We were all black, we were all young, and we were all trying to tell stories we thought worth telling." As Terry worked to perfect her craft, she never knew what response to expect from Leonard. Some days he was encouraging; other days he was jealous and frustrated. Then in the summer of 1983, Terry discovered that she was pregnant. In spite of the instability of her relationship with Leonard, Terry decided to keep the baby. On April 24, 1984, Terry gave birth to a baby boy whom she named Solomon Welch. Leonard was with her during the delivery. Terry asked Doris Jean Austin to be Solomon's godmother.

Thrilled with her young son, Terry nonetheless realized that her relationship with the baby's father was coming to an end when he hit her for the second time. "You know how people lift cars on the freeway?" Terry asked in an interview with *Ebony* in which she recounted the experience. "I got strong. He couldn't believe it. I jumped on him and grabbed him by the neck and threw him up against the bed. And I told him, 'If you ever put your hands on me again, I'm not going to be one of these women who call the police and the next thing you know you can come back home. I will press charges and you will go to jail.'"

Terry had learned from years of watching her mother and father that allowing a man to abuse her could only lead to pain and heartache. Before Solomon turned a year old, Terry had severed all ties to Leonard Welch. "When I became the brunt of his anger, I had to really stop and think about my own well-being and the future of my son," she has explained. "Both were at stake and I chose me and my son."

Perhaps in part because her home life was more settled, Terry decided to focus on marketing her writing. She gathered up all her short stories and sent them to Houghton Mifflin, the publisher of Ann Petry's 1946 novel *The Street,* which Terry had admired back in college. "I decided I had nothing to lose by sending [them the] stories," Terry said. "I thought, maybe I'll get some free editorial advice." In the cover letter that accompanied her collection, she also mentioned that she had written a novel.

Terry never expected the response she received. While Houghton loved the stories, the publisher explained that collections of short stories were difficult to market. However, they wanted to see the novel she had mentioned. Terry was scared. For one thing, the approximately 400-page manuscript was in rough shape because she had been focusing so much energy on her short stories. How would a publisher evaluate a story that was in such ragged form? Setting aside her fears of rejection, she sent the novel in anyway.

About four days later she got a letter from Houghton Mifflin. It included an offer to buy the book and publish it in hardback. Terry was stunned. "I freaked out," she recalled. "I got knots in my stomach at the thought of how much I had to revise."

Lawrence Kessenich, an editor at Houghton at that time, contacted Terry. "I talked to Terry," he explained. "I don't really remember that clearly that initial conversation, but of course she was very excited and quite interested. And you know the routine of a publishing house, I had to give it to a lot of other people to read. And those people liked it and thought it was worth taking on.

"So we took it on," Kessenich continued. "I can't recall the exact figure, but it was a fairly typical advance for a first novel that you didn't expect to be something that was going to break out of the pack in some big way, so it was around $4,000 or $5,000, something like that. . . . I told her she should get an agent so she would know what the general situation was with first novels. So she got an agent, Diane Cleaver." While Cleaver was a highly experienced agent, Terry sensed over time that the suggested revisions showed that the woman didn't really understand what Terry was trying to do. Eventually she changed agents.

The editors at Houghton were impressed with how willing Terry was to make changes and revisions. She got up early in the morning so that she could put in three to four hours of writing before dropping off Solomon at the babysitter and taking the subway downtown to whichever law office she was working at that day. But through all the additions and revisions Terry made to what had once been a simple college short story, her original vision never changed: she was exploring how a black woman on her own had raised five children.

As the book neared the final stages of editing, Lawrence Kessenich had a conversation with Terry in which he explained that publishing houses do not spend much money promoting first novels. Terry, who had visions of 20-city book tours, was stunned. But then Kessenich suggested that she try an approach that he had used with another first-time author. That writer had sent postcards with personal notes to hundreds of booksellers throughout the country. The man's book sales were slightly higher than normal for a first novel, and Kessenich thought Terry would have an even greater advantage because she was an African-American woman. Novels by black women were not as common as those written by white men.

In an article first published in *Poets & Writers Magazine*, she described her feelings when she learned how little her publisher would do to promote the book. "I was disappointed and hurt, but more than anything, I felt I'd been misled by them. After all, hadn't my editor exclaimed his excitement over my book? And hadn't they sent me their booklet, 'A Guide for Authors,' telling me the various ways in which they would determine the most appropriate strategy for drawing attention to my book?"

A quick check with other writers made Terry realize that this treatment was not at all unusual. Unless a first-time novelist has an established audience or knows all the right people in the industry, publishing houses typically do not devote much time or money to publicizing the work. But she also wondered if being black had more to do with it than being a first-time writer.

Terry was determined not to let the system block her path to success. "I had worked hard on my novel and I wanted as many people as possible to know that it existed," she wrote. "I'd heard too many horror stories about first novels never being reviewed, never being available in bookstores. Most terrifying of all to me was the thought of being remaindered, reviewers panning my novel and thus, my never selling enough copies of my book to see a royalty check. I didn't want to be one of those writers, and I also didn't want to spend another year

Mama

Terry McMillan

a novel

Terry's first published novel, Mama, is a fictionalized tribute to one of the hardest-working African-American women she has known—Madeline, Terry's mother.

as a freelance word processor for a law firm in Manhattan."

Terry understood that unless her sales exceeded the publisher's expectations, she wasn't likely to see any more money from *Mama* than the advance check she had already received. Writers typically are paid royalties, a percentage of the money earned from the sales of their books. When a publisher gives a writer an advance, that money is actually royalty payments being received in advance of the publication of the book. Royalties from the actual sales of the book are kept by the publisher until the amount earned by the writer exceeds the advance the publisher has already paid. Terry figured that the only way she was going to get larger than expected sales of *Mama* was by becoming her own publicist.

So she took Lawrence Kessenich's advice about publicity to heart and went even further. Over the next six months, Terry sent out more than 4,000 letters during off hours at the law firms where she worked. She wrote to the sales reps who would be marketing her book to the booksellers, telling them how much she appreciated their efforts on her behalf. Realizing that her primary audience would be black women, she went to the library and got a list of all the black organizations in the United States, as well as the more than 500 women's studies programs at colleges and universities and all the black newspapers, magazines, and radio and TV programs. She got listings of black colleges and African-American studies programs. Not wanting to rely solely on the sales reps to sell her books, she created a list of more than 1,000 bookstores in her home state of Michigan and in cities with large African-American populations.

Then she sent letters to every organization on her lists, telling them about her soon-to-be-released novel. In her letters, she gave the name of her book and who was publishing it. She explained that she was hoping they would order her book, invite her to read from it or give a lecture, use it as a text in their class, or whatever else might be appropriate for the particular organization. Terry's three-year-old son Solomon became part of the operation by using a sponge to seal the envelopes. Over a six-month period, she spent about $700 to publicize her first novel.

The result of Terry's hard work was that by January 14, 1987, the day before her publication date, the first printing of the book had already sold out. She was a guest on seven television shows and six radio shows and was interviewed for more than a dozen newspapers. *Mama* was reviewed in more than 30 magazines and newspapers, and most of the reviews were positive. William Blythe, writing in the *New York Times*, observed, "In its inexorable movement toward economic doom, 'Mama' distinguishes itself by its exuberant comic sensibility, proving that dignity can't be carried in a wallet. When life presses in on Mildred in the form of bill collectors, police and nosey neighbors, she presses right back." Many reviewers picked up on the fact that while Alice Walker, the acclaimed African-American author of *The Color Purple*, and Terry McMillan both wrote about life as a poor black woman in America, Walker described how things used to be. *Mama* described things as they are.

Terry dedicated the novel with these words: "For my own Mama, Madeline Tillman, whose love and support made everything possible." In her acknowledgments, she thanked Kessenich for his encouragement and reassurance. She also included the poem "When I Have Reached the Point of Suffocation" by Gerald Stern, which explores making your life new in the face of the destruction of beautiful things. In many ways, the poem described what Terry was trying to do with her own life.

Author Alice Walker's subject matter is similar to Terry McMillan's, but her approach is different. Walker writes about black women of earlier generations. McMillan's emphasis is on the contemporary lives of black women.

Terry learned from her experience in marketing Mama *that contact with her readers is important to the success of her books.*

It was important to Terry to involve her son, Solomon, in this big event. "Around my publication date," she wrote in *Poets and Writers Magazine*, "my three-year-old son and I spent days gallivanting around Brooklyn and Manhattan to bookstores to see if they had *Mama* on their shelves. The shocker was that most of them did, and when I told them I was the author all of them asked me to autograph the books!"

Within six weeks, *Mama* was in its third printing. Terry's publisher was both shocked and pleased. Until that time, U.S. publishers assumed that it was close to impossible to market books to African-American readers, so they didn't bother trying. Terry single-handedly changed that perception. Suddenly they realized that black readers were willing to buy books, and that grass-roots appearances like the ones Terry had arranged were among the most effective ways to create a market for books by African-American writers.

Excited as Terry was by the largely positive reception *Mama* was getting, she also responded to critics. Some people assumed that the book was totally autobiographical, and even one of Terry's relatives took offense at what she wrote. "Some events in the book really happened," Terry replied. "There are the same number of children in my family, I moved to California when I was seventeen, my mother and my two sisters came, my brother has been to prison, he did use dope at one point. I used to drink. But I don't drink any more, and I depict Freda as this lush. My brother asked me if I had ever been raped and the answer is no. One of my aunts thinks she's in the book and is not speaking to me. My mother is not an alcoholic. What I did was take my experience and exaggerate it. Everybody's work is autobiographical, despite what they say."

She also corrected people who complained that the book created an unflattering portrayal of black people. "This book is not meant to represent or portray any gender or group of people," she explained. "Nobody thinks that a Czech writer is representing all Czechs, or a Russian writer is writing for all Russians."

Because the book sold better than Houghton had expected, Terry had soon paid back her advance. Royalty checks began arriving every few months. While Terry was finally earning money from her book, it certainly wasn't enough to retire on. So she continued writing.

Terry was pleased with how her first novel was doing, but she was still set on doing something other than secretarial work to help pay her bills. And at about that time, her friend and mentor Ishmael Reed came through with a job offer that appealed to her in an unique way.

7
STARTING OVER

❦

THE YEAR BEFORE *Mama* came out, Ishmael Reed had read some of his poetry at the University of Wyoming in Laramie. While there, he learned that the English faculty was looking for a writing teacher who would be willing to move to Wyoming. Because of frequent phone calls from Terry, Reed knew that she was tired of working in law firms but that she wanted a solid financial foundation for herself and her son. He immediately recommended Terry for the teaching position.

Terry had never taught before, but that didn't bother Ishmael Reed. "I knew by the manuscripts she was sending me that she was ready," he said. "She knew her way around. I mean, Terry's very forceful and she's very articulate. I figured that after all these years of writing and attending these workshops and everything, she could teach a course in writing. She knew the strategies and the mechanics of it. So I told them that I had a perfect candidate."

Lisa Shipley, assistant to the head of the English department at the university, described the type of position Terry was hired for. "At that time we had twenty-eight or twenty-nine tenure track faculty members. . . . We had lecturers also, part-time people. They taught full time but were considered part time because their positions didn't necessarily continue. They were generally one-year appointments. Terry's was a temporary one-year appointment. . . .

A teaching appointment at the University of Wyoming in Laramie broadened Terry's personal and professional horizons, literally and figuratively.

[The requirements are] based more on record than on education. If you were looking for someone to teach Shakespeare, you would look for more education than research or publication. But with creative writing we look more for the record, that is, your publications." Terry's experience at Yaddo and MacDowell and the publication of *Mama* provided Terry with the necessary credentials.

Terry herself had some questions about going to Wyoming. "I knew I wanted to leave Brooklyn—but Wyoming?" she wrote in the "Letters from Home" section of *Wigwag* magazine. But when she got a phone call offering a position at the university and a paid invitation to go out to Laramie and look the situation over, she figured she didn't have anything to lose.

Laramie, Wyoming, was a totally different world from New York City, but in many ways it reminded Terry of Port Huron. About 35,000 people lived in the area, and its downtown was only about two blocks long. "I felt like I'd been thrown back in time about forty years," she said. "All the little stores looked hopeless, as if they were begging for business. There was one shoe store, and a J. C. Penney whose mannequins still wore their hair in starched pageboys and whose hands reached out for something that wasn't there. Sears was just a counter where you could order things from the catalog."

The area was also predominantly white. She heard that there were 62 black people who lived in Laramie, but she saw few of them. Cultural events were hard to come by. Terry recognized that she was considering a major change in lifestyle.

After going home to Brooklyn and giving it serious thought, she decided to accept the position and moved to Wyoming in time for the fall term of 1987. Ishmael Reed admired her for taking the plunge. "It takes spunk to do that," he said, "to get out of the ethnic cocoon, to go to places like that.

She always had spunk. You go to some of these western towns and you're the only black person there. . . . She went to Laramie and those people fell in love with her. She was a good teacher and they wanted to keep her. I heard from them, and they were very satisfied with her. They wanted her to stay there, and they wanted to give her tenure. I think that was a terrific experience for her."

One of the advantages of life in Wyoming that Terry quickly discovered was that housing was much less expensive than in New York City. For a rent of $515 a month, Terry and Solomon moved into a 2,100-square-foot, three-bedroom, two-bathroom duplex that included a huge family room with a wood-burning stove, a living room with a working fireplace, a dining room, a back deck, and a 180-degree view of the mountains in the Medicine Bow National Forest.

Terry traded Brooklyn's brownstones and busy beat for Wyoming's inspirational but occasionally isolating beauty. This picture is of Medicine Bow National Forest.

She put Solomon in preschool and was amazed at the quality care it provided for less than $150 a month. The 14 children had three teachers and played in an 8,000-square-foot playground. "Every Monday they got swimming lessons," she said. "Wednesdays they went roller-skating, and Thursdays they'd go on field trips. Solomon was three and a half and could say his numbers and colors in Spanish. . . . I was starting to like it here."

Things were also progressing professionally for Terry. That year she got a new agent, courtesy of a recommendation from Lawrence Kessenich. Literary agent Molly Friedrich arrived on the scene just in

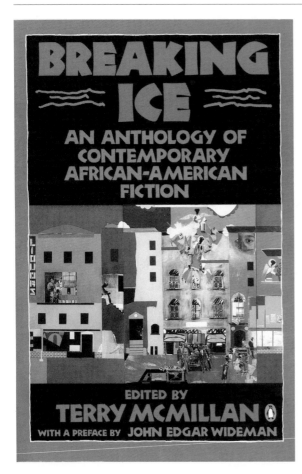

Terry's choice of title for Breaking Ice *represents the struggle by writers of color for publication and positive recognition of their writing.*

time for the negotiations that were taking place as Houghton Mifflin sold the paperback rights for *Mama*. She insisted that Houghton ask for more money, and the larger payment came through.

Terry had received a 1986 New York Foundation for the Arts fellowship and the Doubleday/Columbia University Literary fellowship. Because of her visibility, she was also asked to review books for the *Atlanta Constitution*, the *Philadelphia Inquirer*, and the *New York Times Book Review*. She began work on her second novel, *A Day Late and a Dollar Short*. Like *Mama*, it focused on a black mother, this time a character named Viola Price.

Terry took her teaching assignment at the university seriously, and she loved the interaction with her students. But it didn't take her long to discover that people of color were not well represented in the standard college anthologies. "It just hit me," she said. "There are no black writers, no Third World writers." Never one to sit idly by, she quickly researched the market and created a proposal for an anthology of contemporary black writers.

Accepted by Penguin for publication, the collection was titled *Breaking Ice: An Anthology of Contemporary African-American Fiction*. In the introduction, Terry explained how the idea of the name came to her: "I was looking out my window at the snow piled up, the thick icicles hanging off the house, and I thought about how . . . as African-American writers we have . . . been breaking ice not only in getting published, but [in] getting the respect and attention our work deserves."

Much as Terry loved her work and the people in Laramie, by the end of 1987, she was starting to be reminded a little too much of her childhood in Port Huron. The town was small. She was tired of the cold and the long winter. And she was bored. Struck with cabin fever and enduring the third day of being home with Solomon while both of them recovered from a virus, Terry heard the phone ring. The call was from the University of Arizona, asking if she would be interested in a teaching job. Terry's first question was not about salary. Instead she asked what the temperature was that day. "Seventy-five," came the response.

"I looked at the frost on the windows, at my $281 heating bill, and said yes," she recounted. On May 24, 1988, Terry notified her friends that she had accepted a position as associate professor of creative writing at the University of Arizona and that she and Solomon would be leaving for Tucson on June 1.

Although the population of Tucson was around 600,000, in many ways it reminded Terry of a small town. Unlike her days in Los Angeles or New York City, she was very much a member of a minority. Only 3 percent of the population in Tucson was African American. She had a hard time finding interesting dates, and this became a theme in articles she wrote during this period.

In an article for the "Hers" feature in the *New York Times*, Terry described her ideal—but unattainable—man as "a black man who feels good enough about himself so that he's not threatened by me. That he's not out to control or mold me. . . . In the dream, he laughs a lot. In the dream he's smart. In the dream he loves children. In the dream he's physical. In the dream we love each other, treat each other with kindness and respect."

In spite of the frustrations she felt about her social life, Terry enjoyed teaching, and the weather in Arizona was much more comfortable than it had been in Wyoming. She also took the major step of becoming a home owner. Because of the salary she made at the university, she needed a tax shelter so she began looking for a house. She settled on a place in a new development with an award-winning school district and a magnificent view of the mountains.

As she had done in the past, Terry began using her life experiences as the basis for her writing. Thinking about her relationship with Solomon's father and the things that had gone wrong, she began writing a novel about a stormy relationship between Zora Banks, a middle-class black woman working to become a songwriter, and Franklin Smith, a high school dropout and building contractor who is usually unemployed and has a drug problem. The book is told from both characters' perspectives. One chapter is written from Zora's point of view; the next chapter is told by Franklin.

"I was trying to understand what happened in my relationship," Terry explained. "I fell in love with a man who was not as educated as I am. The problems in the relationship come from the bad decisions this man made because of his hang-ups. I wanted to put myself in this man's shoes, to see his side of the story. In every relationship there are two sides to every story. When you're honest you don't have anything to lose."

Because her contract for *Mama* with Houghton Mifflin gave that publisher the right to see her next novel before any other publisher, Terry sent part of the manuscript to Houghton. Negotiations over the manuscript dissolved. Terry and her agent, Molly Friedrich, wanted a $20,000 advance based on about the first 100 pages of the novel. Houghton was conservative and didn't like the idea of committing that much money to an unfinished manuscript. As Larry Kessenich explained, "I didn't feel like the content was hopeless. I just felt like I needed to see what the novel was going to be like. I'd seen many novels, even ones that started out really well, that fell apart in the second half. And I had some doubts even about how this one had started out. It wasn't that I was definitely saying no, I was just saying 'I need to see the rest of the novel.'"

Terry and Molly, however, thought an advance should be offered based on the quality and sales of *Mama*. Terry viewed Houghton's reservations as a sign that the publisher didn't believe in her ability as a writer. She also thought that the editors didn't understand the variety of individuals within the black community. "They weren't acknowledging that we had other experiences," she said. "Everything was supposed to be racially motivated. We don't just fall in love and get our hearts broken just like everybody else. No, there's got to be something about being exploited. I'm sorry I did not make Zora barefoot, pregnant, getting . . . kicked in the projects. But that's not the story I wanted to tell."

When the situation with Houghton didn't work, Kessenich was philosophical. "I knew enough about the plight of authors," he said. "If they feel like they're not supported, they have to go somewhere where they can get a better deal. Publishing houses are perfectly willing to let *them* go, so there's no reason why they shouldn't be willing to let the publishing house go."

Terry's agent, Molly Friedrich, immediately sent the sample chapters to Viking Penguin. Within two days, Penguin purchased the book. *Disappearing Acts*, as Terry had titled her second published book, was released in August 1989. On the 11th of that month, she sent a signed copy of the book to Solomon's father, Leonard Welch. She enclosed a letter in which she cautioned him, "Don't read this like it's YOUR biography or YOUR story. . . . Try to read it as

While living in Tucson, Terry began work on her second novel, Disappearing Acts. *Although based on her life in New York with Leonard Welch, it is not an autobiography.*

fiction, because I took liberties in order to make the story more plausible."

While *Mama* initially had sold tens of thousands of copies, *Disappearing Acts* sold several hundred thousand copies. Terry once again dedicated herself to publicizing the book, giving readings, signing books at stores, and appearing on television and radio programs. MGM bought the movie rights to the book and contracted Terry to write the screenplay.

Readers loved the book, although they didn't always agree with the decisions the main characters made. David Nicholson, writing in the *Washington Post Book World*, pointed out that while having a romantic interest between characters from widely differing worlds is an old, established plot line, it rings particularly true with African Americans. He wrote, "Professional black women complain of an ever-shrinking pool of eligible men, citing statistics that show the number of black men in prison is increasing, while the number of black men in college is decreasing. Articles on alternatives for women, from celibacy to . . . relationships with blue-collar workers like Franklin have long been a staple of black general interest and women's magazines."

Many critics were impressed with Terry's ability to give the character of Franklin a true, believable voice. Many also complained about the amount of profanity in *Disappearing Acts*. "But in her effort to achieve authenticity," a critic wrote in *Publishers Weekly*, "the author bombards readers with four-letter words, and the effect is both irritating and distancing." Valerie Sayers, writing in the *New York Times Book Review*, complained, "Zora's voice is way too flat. Even her profanity gets boring. Franklin's profanity also gets old." And in a generally positive review from *Washington Post Book World*, David Nicholson wrote, "What's troublesome is the abundant profanity—as much as one obscenity every other line on some pages—so much that it soon becomes neither funny nor shocking, but merely tedious."

Terry McMillan disagrees. "Sometimes you get these real prissy types who pretend like they've never heard any of these words, and they say, 'I don't know why Miss McMillan felt she had to portray black women speaking such vulgarities,'" she said in an interview in the *New York Times*. "But the truth is, if you eavesdrop on people's conversations, we abuse language. We don't always speak correctly, and we often use words that we wouldn't want our children to use. And, girl, this book isn't about how we would like to see life. It's about how life really is."

But the question of how closely her fiction matched real life was about to become a legal issue. As Terry McMillan began the new year of 1990, she had no way of knowing that Leonard Welch was angry about the character of Franklin Swift in *Disappearing Acts*. He was so angry, in fact, that he was about to seek legal action.

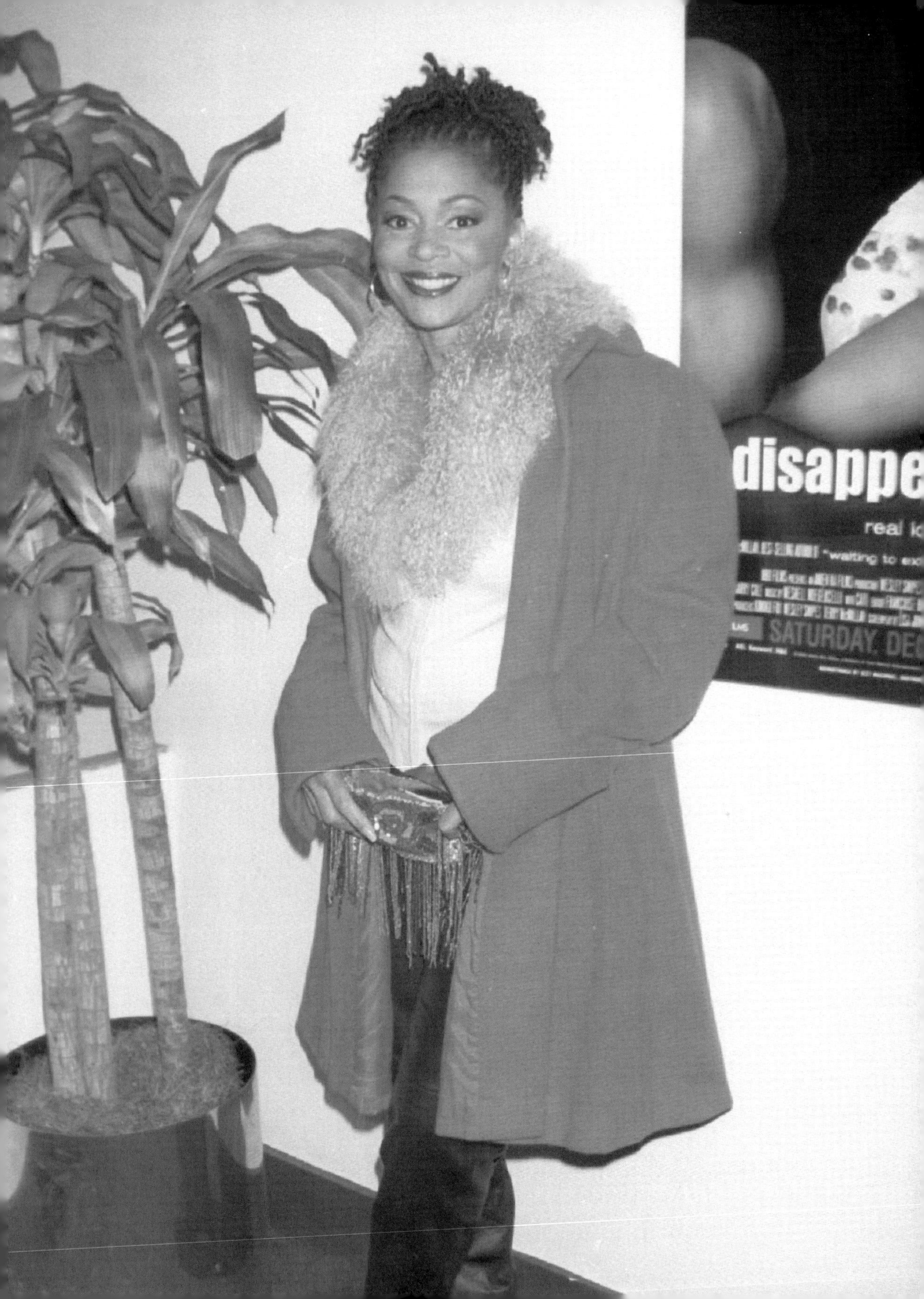
disappe
real lo
SATURDAY, DE

8

CONFLICT OF INTERESTS

❦

WHEN LEONARD WELCH first received a copy of *Disappearing Acts* from Terry, he immediately recognized similarities between himself and the character Franklin. Like Leonard, Franklin had dropped out of high school and earned a high school equivalency diploma. The two men were construction workers who did carpentry on the side. They had the same complexion, height, weight, hair, and mustache. Just like Leonard, Franklin had a trick knee, a habit of drip-drying after the shower, and a love of working out at the gym. They even liked the same breakfast food.

The similarities didn't stop there. The character of Franklin met his girlfriend Zora the same way Leonard had met Terry. The fictional couple and real-life couple had their first argument over the same thing—a revealing bathing suit. The characters in the book moved to a brownstone similar to the one Franklin and Terry had lived in. They even took a trip to Saratoga Springs, New York, that was almost identical to a trip Franklin and Terry had taken.

But then reality and fiction parted ways. The character Franklin Swift turned out to be an alcoholic who drank on the job, and hated white people and gays. He was a rapist. He took drugs. He didn't go to work because he was lazy and was happy to live off Zora.

Leonard Welch became quite upset. He was afraid friends would recognize him in the book and

Disappearing Acts would lead to both public and private problems for Terry McMillan when Leonard Welch filed a lawsuit against her for defamation of character. Welch claimed that the character of Franklin Swift in the novel was recognizable as Welch and portrayed him in a negative way.

73

think that he, too, was an alcoholic and a drug addict who hated white people and gays and raped women. He decided to consult lawyer Peter S. Gordon, a member of Bedell & Feinberg. Welch asked if the attorney thought he had a case against Terry McMillan. Gordon thought that he did.

In August 1990, the attorney filed a defamation lawsuit against Terry, her publisher Viking Penguin, and Simon & Schuster, the publishing house that issued the paperback edition of *Disappearing Acts*. The lawsuit charged that the main character in the novel, Franklin Swift, was recognizably Leonard Welch and that the depiction of Welch's three-year relationship with Terry along with the fact that the novel was dedicated to their son, Solomon, caused him emotional distress. It asked for $4,750,000 in return. The complaint went on for 28 pages, itemizing each instance in the book that defamed Welch and placing a dollar value on each such passage.

News of the lawsuit alarmed fiction writers and publishers nationwide. The ruling made in this lawsuit could be used as a precedent, affecting any other writer. Novelist Marita Golden said that the case was frightening "because some of the greatest fiction is based on real people. I think it's just part of the general nastiness of the time that people see someone doing well and they want part of it. It's part of the whole intolerance of the imagination." She added that if Welch won, "it would definitely [have] a chilling effect on fiction writers."

Viking Penguin was determined to fight back. Their attorney, Martin Garbus, had 30 years of experience handling freedom-of-speech cases. On the advice of their respective attorneys, neither Terry nor Leonard said anything in public about the case while the lawsuit was pending. They waited in silence for months as pages of motions, stipulations, and affidavits were filed back and forth.

Meanwhile, Terry began promotional activities for her anthology *Breaking Ice,* which was released in 1990. Writer Joyce Carol Oates reviewed the book for the *Washington Post Books World,* describing it as "a wonderfully generous and diverse collection of prose fiction by our most gifted African-American writers." She also praised the job Terry had done in selecting the contents of the anthology, which contained such "high quality of writing . . . that one could hardly distinguish between the categories [of writers] in terms of origi-

Despite a hectic schedule of teaching and writing, Terry welcomed her mother Madeline Tillman to Tucson in 1990. Tillman moved from Los Angeles with the hope that the climate change would improve her asthma.

nality, depth of vision and command of the language."

Terry also welcomed her mother to the Tucson area that year. Madeline Tillman had decided to move to the desert from Los Angeles because she had developed asthma. A chronic condition, asthma causes the air passages in a person's lungs both to tighten on the outside and swell on the inside. During a full-blown asthma attack, a person has great difficulty breathing. Without proper treatment, asthma attacks can lead to death. Air pollution and allergens in Los Angeles had aggravated her condition, even with the medication she took, and she hoped the dry, cleaner air of the Arizona desert would help her breathe more easily.

Terry was glad to be close to her mother again, but her schedule was becoming increasingly hectic as was life with energetic six-year-old Solomon. She was working on her next novel, *Waiting to Exhale,* which was due to the publisher by September 1, 1991. She was continuing to teach, and that year she had been honored by being asked to be one of a five-member panel of judges that would choose the National Book Award winner in the fiction category. The National Book Awards are given out each year to "recognize books of exceptional merit written by Americans" in the categories of poetry, fiction, non-fiction, and young people's literature. The winner in each category receives a $10,000 cash award and a crystal sculpture.

Throughout the summer of 1990, Terry received packages from publishers with copies of the 375 books they wanted considered for the fiction award. By October, she and the other four judges were supposed to have read all the titles and narrowed the submissions down to five finalists. The other judges were three men and another woman, Catharine Stimpson, who also chaired the committee. All of the panelists had backgrounds in education and fiction writing. Terry was the youngest of the group and the only African American.

She also understood that the National Book Awards seemed to always have some controversy attached to them. Three years earlier, in 1987, 48 African-American writers and critics had signed a statement expressing their dismay that the author Toni Morrison had not won a National Book Award. Their statement appeared in the *New York Times Book Review*. Critic Houston A. Baker Jr. and poet June Jordan, in a letter published with the statement, pointed out that James Baldwin had never received either the National Book Award or the Pulitzer Prize. "We grieve," they wrote, "because we cannot yet assure that such shame, such national neglect, will not occur again, and then, again."

In the context of this larger controversy, a division developed among the five judges in 1990. On November 27, 1990, the day the winners were to be selected during a committee meeting in New York City, a *New York Times* article reported that the

Charles Johnson receives the 1990 National Book Award for his novel, Middle Passage. *Terry McMillan was one of five judges for the award.*

judges were split by "deep ideological divisions," reflecting the recent changes in the publishing industry. "I came out of the selection process for finalists feeling that only a couple of the five books represent my tastes, preferences, and standards," committee member Paul West complained.

But when the one winner among the five finalists was chosen, the committee gave the 1990 National Book Award for fiction to Charles Johnson for his book *Middle Passage*. In 40 years, this was only the fourth time a black writer had received a National Book Award. Previous winners were Ralph Ellison, for *Invisible Man*; Gloria Naylor, for *The Women of Brewster Place*; and Alice Walker, for *The Color Purple*.

Opponents of the selection complained when Terry stood up and cheered as the prize was announced at a ceremony at the Plaza Hotel. The *New Republic* called her "a mediocre novelist whose work is consecrated to the spirits of women and blacks" and charged her with calling a white judge a racist.

Once the awards ceremony was over, Terry returned to Arizona to continue teaching and working

feverishly on her novel *Waiting to Exhale*. As was her
habit, she got the idea for the book from her own life.
"That's what prompted me to write this story," she
explained in an interview in *Ebony*. "I started asking
myself, '*What am I doing wrong* [in my relationships
with men]?' And then I started thinking, 'Wait a
minute. I'm not alone out here." The story is set in
Arizona and features four black women who are successful in their professional lives but have terrible relationships with men.

By the beginning of 1991, Terry realized she was
working too hard. Caring for Solomon, the pressures
of the lawsuit, having less than eight months to fin-
ish her novel, and publicity work for *Disappearing
Acts* and *Breaking Ice* left her exhausted. She decided
to take a leave of absence from the University of Arizona after the end of the spring 1991 semester.

On April 3, some of the pressure was eased when
Judge Jules L. Spodek dismissed the defamation lawsuit against Terry and her publishers. The judge
found that while the character Franklin Swift was an
abusive drunk who was racist, lazy, hostile toward
women and gays, and emotionally unbalanced,
"Leonard Welch is none of these things." The judge
observed that people who knew Welch "had no difficulty differentiating him from Franklin Swift; the
defamatory material was clearly not believed." The
judge noted that it was accepted practice for writers
to create fiction from their lives, and that before
defamation could be proven, a reader would have to
be totally convinced that a character in a book "is
not fiction at all."

Allowed to speak publicly about the case for the
first time, Terry said, "Undoubtedly I am quite
relieved, not just for myself but for other writers. I
created a fictional character for which he was par-
tially the inspiration. But, it is fiction. You make it
up. This was a love story, written with love, and he
knows it."

During her leave of absence from the University of Arizona, Terry decided to move back to California, although her mother chose to stay in Tucson where her health was so much improved. As soon as spring term finished, Terry began packing things up, being careful to keep her computer out until the last possible moment so that she could get as much work done on *Waiting to Exhale* as possible. "I had the movers take my computer last," she said. "They were putting books in boxes, and I was sitting there writing. I get to California, I'm sitting in my sister's fiancé's office going blind writing on my little laptop that's not backlit, I'm looking for a place to live while my furniture's on a truck somewhere, it's the end of August, and I'm supposed to be finishing the book by September 1!"

Needless to say, Terry didn't make her deadline, and for someone who placed a priority on being prompt, this was a big disappointment. She also was thrown into a depression when she turned 40 that October. "Worrying about aging became this kind of obsession," she admitted in an interview with *Ebony*. "All of a sudden little bags under my eyes seemed huge. And I started thinking, 'You'll never have another baby now, forget it.'"

Wanting to make sure the finished manuscript would be in as good shape as possible, she sent copies of finished parts of the book to her friend Doris Jean Austin, knowing that Doris would give her a professional, honest critique. The finished manuscript was sent to Viking in December. Having dedicated her first novel to her mother and her second to her son, she decided to dedicate *Waiting to Exhale* to her father: "This one's for you, Daddy: Edward Lewis McMillan, 1929–1968."

As the book went through the editing process, Terry was struck by an idea for the cover art. A year before she had purchased a painting by Synthia St. James. Titled *Ensemble*, it showed a group of regal women—perfect to represent the main characters in

Racial tensions exploded into street riots in spring 1992, following the acquittal of four white police officers. The officers were charged with police brutality against black motorist Rodney King.

Terry's book. St. James gave her permission, and her artwork was used on the covers of later paperback editions of Terry's fiction as well.

By the beginning of 1992, bidding wars had begun between movie studios for the film rights to *Waiting to Exhale*. At first, Terry wasn't very interested in the idea of her book being turned into a movie. She didn't see how it could be done well. But then she realized that as a love story, it would be a welcome change from the standard action-adventure treatment Hollywood gave to any movies that predominantly featured African Americans. In an interview with the *New York Times*, she said, "What's important to me is that a movie like this gets on the screen because we black people have to see ourselves as sensuous, erotic, passionate beings on the screen, like white people do. We never get that opportunity."

The movie rights went to Twentieth Century Fox, and Terry reportedly was paid a fee "comfortably" into the six figures. The movie studio asked her to write the screenplay, but Terry wasn't excited about that idea. She had struggled to write the screenplay for *Disappearing Acts*, and the movie still hadn't been produced. So she declined the offer and suggested that Fox get another writer. She would still be able to approve the finished screenplay.

That spring, national events grabbed Terry's attention. Her awareness of civil rights and social action had come a long way since the days when she lived in Port Huron. So when an all-white jury acquitted four police officers of the beating of African-American Rodney King in April 1992, Terry felt she had to do something. She sat down and wrote an op-ed piece for the *New York Times,* which was published on May 1, 1992. In it, she assailed the injustices she saw regularly in America. "My brother is in prison right now," she wrote. "He was arrested 10 miles from Simi Valley for drunk driving. Fortunately, he didn't get beaten. How many white men have gone to jail for the same offense? How many innocent black men who have been beaten never made it on videotape? And now, what difference would it make?"

At the conclusion of her piece, she called for people to be exposed to new experiences so that they could better understand each other's actions and work for justice: "My brother should be back at work. Those jurors should be forced to know what it feels like to be kicked and hit with a baton while lying on concrete. And those policemen should've been behind bars a long time ago. Praying for guidance. Something. A conscience maybe."

Although she hadn't planned it, Terry's book *Waiting to Exhale* was about to stir up other issues within the African-American community.

9

BREATHING ROOM

—— ❦ ——

N O ONE WAS prepared for the huge commercial success that followed the May 28, 1992, hardcover release of *Waiting to Exhale*. Obviously Viking expected it to have respectable sales. The first printing was 85,000 copies, and unlike the days when Terry was single-handedly marketing *Mama*, this time Viking had arranged a huge 26-city, six-week book tour.

The tour began with Terry giving a breakfast speech at the annual American Booksellers Association convention in Anaheim, California. It ended in July with a reading in New York City at Central Park's Summer Stage festival. In between, Terry spoke at close to 30 bookstores, including a stop in her hometown of Port Huron, Michigan.

People mobbed her book signings: 1,200 in Chicago, 1,000 in Washington. According to Waldenbooks, police were used at a signing on the edge of South-Central Los Angeles to control the huge crowd. When Terry gave readings, she said she felt like she was a preacher at a revival meeting. A writer for the *New York Times* reported that hours before Terry's scheduled appearance at a reading at the Hirshhorn Museum in Washington, her readers—mostly black women students, professionals, and homemakers—lined up. Then when Terry began to read, the crowd joined in. "You can say that again, sister!" someone called out. Other responses quickly spread through the crowd.

"It doesn't get much better than that, hearing that kind of reaction to your book," Terry later said. "It feels like being in church. You know, we have this call-and-response thing in the black church, people crying out when the preacher talks. 'Yes, I hear you! You're talking to me!' Black audiences let you know how they feel. They don't hold back. . . . I love it."

In each city, the publisher hired people to pick Terry up at her hotel and drive her to her scheduled appearances. One of these assistants, an African-American woman, told Terry, "Girl, I don't know what your next book is going to be about, but please, please, I beg you, don't start going all deep on us. Please don't start floating and decide now you're going to write the book of life. Please keep doing it the way you've been doing it and tell us the stories that we can relate to because that's what we need, so don't start switching up on us."

Many readers shared the woman's love for Terry's writing. By the end of 1992, more than 700,000 hardcover copies of *Waiting to Exhale* had been sold, and that figure reached 800,000 before the paperback version was released. The paperback rights were sold by the publisher to Pocket Books for $2.64 million. At the time, it was a record figure for any novel written by an African American and one of the highest amounts paid to any writer, regardless of race.

Of course, not everyone was quite as enthusiastic about the book. Frances Stead Sellers reviewed it for the *Times Literary Supplement* and compared it to "the type of sexy, popular novel that has been making Jilly Cooper and Danielle Steel rich for years." She went on to observe, "Whether her views are politically correct or not, McMillan has hit a nerve. Many African-American women identify with her heroines. . . . Its one true importance is that it appeals to a market that American publishers have previously overlooked—the new black middle class. But its literary merits are modest."

Many reviewers once again complained about the profanity in her books and grew weary of the constant use of brand names. Instead of a breath mint, Savannah sucked on a Tic Tac. She also "splashed on puddles of Joy" rather than simply using perfume. Defenders argued that brand names were more precise than generic names and gave a sense of the socioeconomic level of the characters.

Because the male characters were drug addicts, liars, or egomaniacs, some people complained that Terry was bashing African-American men. At one reading when the issue came up, Terry said, "First of all, men need to just grow up." A woman in the back yelled, *"Thank you."* Terry went on to explain her position. "Usually the ones whining and complaining about male-bashing are the ones who're doin' all this [stuff]. I deliberately chose men that women don't need to be bringing home to their mamas. My question was, Why do we pick them?"

In an interview with *Ebony*, she added, "They [the male characters] weren't all dogs. But you have to understand, too, that these women were not exactly saints. Look at Robin. She's a real ditz, a dummy. Her whole world revolves around men, and the men she chooses don't treat her right. It says a lot about how she feels about herself. To make that point, we had to get a man who treated her that way."

Not all African-American men took offense at what she had done, however. The *Los Angeles Times* reported that a black man from an audience of more than 2,000 said, "I think I speak for a lot of brothers. I know I'm all over the book. . . . All I can say is, I'm willing to learn. Being defensive is not the answer."

Others complained that Terry wasn't dealing with serious issues of oppression and victimization. Her fans disagreed. Clara Villarosa, the African-American owner of Hue-Man Experience Bookstore

Terry's books' characters speak in modern style, slang included. Author Toni Morrison writes of black women's struggles in an earlier historical setting and her characters' dialogue reflects earlier patterns of speech.

in Denver, explained the tastes of women who bought *Waiting to Exhale* this way: "When you look at the literature of Toni Morrison or Alice Walker, a lot of it reported on experiences in rural areas, or back when contemporary black fiction, in a black woman's voice, was a total void. These women weren't reading the Toni Morrisons. They'd say, 'Honey, I want it to sound like me.' And when it did, they loved it."

They loved it so much that many African-American women formed "sista circles" where McMillan's books and others like them were read and discussed. Candence Walker, a member of one such group named Sisterfriends, said, "I Love Toni Morrison and Alice Walker, but they can be difficult to understand. I read [Morrison's] 'The Bluest Eye' twice before it made sense, and then I still think I missed some of it. I never had that problem with Terry." Gladys Johns, another member, agreed: "I admire those [writers], but damn, they depress me. I know we've been victims as black women, but Alice and Toni really stick it to you and I don't want to be reminded of it all the time. Terry talks

Although criticized by some for choosing a white Jewish male, Terry's choice of screenwriter Ron Bass to help bring the lives of the four main characters in Waiting to Exhale *to the big screen proved successful.*

about problems, but with humor and fun. I laugh through the tears. That's what I need."

New controversy arose when the screenwriters for the movie version of the novel were announced. Twentieth Century Fox showed Terry the screenplay another writer had done, and she did not like it at all. Then they once again asked her to write the screenplay herself. She agreed, with the stipulation that she be allowed to collaborate with another writer.

In 1993, *The Joy Luck Club*, a movie adaptation of the novel by the same title, became a hit. Terry contacted Amy Tan, the author of the book, and asked her about the experience of adapting her novel for the screen. Amy said it was a largely enjoyable task because she had collaborated with Ron Bass, an experienced screenwriter. "I figured if he could be Chinese, he could be black," Terry said. He accepted her invitation to work with her, and they made a great team.

However, some black critics gave Terry a hard time for choosing to work with a white Jewish male. How could he possibly relate to the black experience?

they wanted to know. The Jewish press had similar questions. In an article in the January 11, 1996, *Metrowest Jewish News*, Bass was asked how an unmarried Jewish man could provide insight into the minds of Asian-American and African-American women. Bass responded that the experiences of the women in *The Joy Luck Club* and in *Waiting to Exhale* were similar to what a lot of women—including Jewish women—went through.

Along with Terry's newfound fame and the controversy surrounding her work came invitations to support just about every charitable organization imaginable. Terry quickly learned an important lesson. "If I said 'yes' to everything I was asked to do, I could forget about writing another book," she said. "For a while, I did say okay and I'd sell tickets or show up at something, but I got burned out. I cannot save the world, which for a while I think I was trying to do. I can't represent every organization, even though I believe in what they're doing. I still have a life."

Part of that life involved finding a home in California in an area where she and Solomon could feel comfortable. After years in Wyoming and Arizona, Terry wanted relatively easy access to city life. She also wanted to be in a good school district for Solomon's benefit, and she felt it was important that there be a number of African-American families in the neighborhood. She stumbled on the perfect spot during her book tour. Driving in the San Francisco Bay Area, Terry got lost and found herself in Danville, California. Thirty miles east of the bay, Danville featured one of the best school districts in the state, as well as athletic and acting programs for kids. The downtown area boasted historic buildings, restaurants, and sidewalk cafes. The town was surrounded by wooded hiking trails and had two parks. Many houses had tremendous views of Mt. Diablo.

In late 1992, Terry purchased a home in Danville. The five-bedroom, gray stucco contemporary house

was at the end of a quiet, dead-end street. From her front porch, she could watch deer on the hills and see horseback riders enjoying the trails. She also counted 23 black families in her neighborhood of more than 100, ensuring that Solomon wouldn't grow up in an all-white environment. Terry immediately felt at home, but she also made some renovations and hired someone to landscape the hill beyond the patio so that it would be full of color.

On all fronts, life was very good for Terry McMillan in 1993. She had financial security, fulfilling work, and a growing reputation in the writing world. "I like myself more now than I did ten years ago," she confided in an interview with *Ebony*, "because there's just too much now that I own." When asked if by that she meant the wealth she finally possessed, she shook her head. "When I say 'own,'" she explained, "I don't mean material things. I mean feeling good about what I'm doing, how I've done it, the changes

In 1992, Terry determined that she and her son Solomon needed a settled home in California where he could go to school and she would have peace to write. She found the small town of Danville, near San Francisco, later that year.

and struggles I've been through. That's what I mean when I say there are certain things I *own* now. Now, I own me."

And Terry didn't entirely turn her back on the needs of others. She sent checks to help support her writer friend Doris Jean Austin, who had recurring health problems. She waived her usual speaking fee (up to $5,000) to teach a single fiction class at an adult-education program in East Harlem. She contributed money to families whom she had never met but whose difficult situations moved her. And she gave generously to her family members.

In September, she decided to surprise her mother by giving her a new car and a house in Tucson. She then left for Rome, to promote *Waiting to Exhale*. On the evening of September 30, Terry called her mother, who was taking care of nine-year-old Solomon while Terry was away. Six hours later, the phone rang. It was a hospital doctor informing Terry that her mother had died during an asthma attack.

Terry was stunned. "I don't think I talked for ten hours after I heard," she said later. She flew back to Port Huron, Michigan, where the funeral was held. Overwhelmed with grief, she was unable to function for 10 months. She felt guilty because she hadn't always empathized with the difficulties her mother experienced from asthma. "Mom's asthma began in adulthood," she explained. "I thought it was psychosomatic."

She couldn't write because the main character in her novel *A Day Late and a Dollar Short* reminded her too much of her mother. She canceled public appearances. "Do you know how hard it is to take your mother out of your address book?" she asked.

Concerned family members and friends sent Terry notes and phoned her regularly. Her best friend Doris Jean Austin, was especially helpful, calling and visiting Terry even though Doris Jean herself wasn't feeling well. Eventually, Terry began to feel some relief from the numbness that had overpowered her for almost a year.

Then, at Terry's encouragement, Doris Jean went to see a doctor. The news was devastating. Doris Jean had terminal, untreatable liver cancer. Terry was again stunned.

Determined to make her friend's last days as joyous as possible, she called Doris Jean from California on the Wednesday before Labor Day and said, "Doris, we're going on a shopping spree, honey. Henri Bendel's. Tiffany's. . . . You wanna go to London? You wanna go to Paris? You wanna go to Africa? Anywhere you wanna go. I'm not kidding. Doris, don't die on me."

The weekend after Labor Day, Doris Jean Austin died. "I couldn't talk or move," Terry said. In less than one year, she had lost the two most important women in the world to her. Terry flew to New York City for the funeral, where she sat in the front row and sobbed. She spent months in denial, hoping that the phone would ring and her mother or Doris Jean would be calling to say it was all a bad joke. But the phone didn't ring, and demands on Terry's time continued.

The Book-of-the-Month Club had bought the rights to Terry's next novel, sight unseen. Terry had been planning to finally complete *A Day Late and a Dollar Short* which she had started right after the publication of *Mama*, and the fact that a major bookclub had bought the rights to the book placed pressure on her to produce.

In November 1994, two months after Doris Jean died, Terry needed to be in Phoenix as the filmmakers scouted locations for shooting *Waiting to Exhale*. Working in the state where her mother had spent her last years brought both sweet and bitter memories to Terry, but she couldn't let that stop her from getting the job done. She was a professional, and she had work to do.

10
CATALYST FOR CHANGE

❦

T HE FILMING OF *Waiting to Exhale* began on February 28, 1995. Before one scene had been shot, the movie had already become the center of controversy. Perhaps because it was the first major motion picture to be based on an African-American woman's novel since the release of *The Color Purple* (Steven Spielberg's movie adapted from Alice Walker's novel), different interest groups wanted to make sure their concerns were recognized.

Not only did Terry receive criticism about her choice of a coscreenwriter, she also heard complaints when Forest Whitaker was chosen as the film's director. Because of the complaints about the alleged "male-bashing" in the novel, she thought people would welcome the movie being directed by an African-American man. She was wrong. She tried to explain her choice.

"I've been approached by people who want to know, 'Why did you get a man to direct *Waiting to Exhale*?' But it's not about gender," she said, "it's about his understanding of the work." She went on to say that she had picked Whitaker because "he's intuitive and sensitive, and he liked those women. He didn't come into the project with some other agenda."

Whitaker himself said, "It's the women in the book who chose certain men who cause them to end up in painful circumstances. As the title suggests, you

The cast of Waiting to Exhale, *from left: Loretta Devine, Whitney Houston, Angela Bassett, and Lela Rochon. The film focuses on the successes and failures of four middle-class black women. It would eventually gross $67 million and prove that there was a market for this type of movie as African-American women lined up at the box office to see it.*

Despite protests from some quarters against Terry's selection of a black male director, Forest Whitaker's sensitive direction contributed to the success of the film.

are talking about people who don't even know how to breathe or feel good about themselves. But luckily, it's the friendship among them that takes them each on a journey of transformation. I never felt like the difficulty of my directing this story is that I'm not a woman. I can only tell the story as I see it and perceive it."

At least people were excited about the four women chosen to portray the main characters. Whitney Houston was cast as Savannah, and Angela Bassett took on the role of Bernadine Harris. Because Whitaker wanted lesser-known black actresses to get some publicity, he gave the role of Robin Stokes to Lela Rochon, who had appeared in the comedies *Boomerang* and *Meteor Man*, and he gave the part of Gloria Johnson to Loretta Devine, who was one of the stars of the Broadway play *Dreamgirls*.

The studio wanted a distinctive soundtrack to help publicize the film and add to its appeal. It hired Kenneth "Babyface" Edmonds to compose and write the soundtrack, which featured Mary J. Blige, Toni Braxton, Aretha Franklin, Chaka Khan, and Patti LaBelle.

Although Terry was welcome to visit the set, she made the trip from California to Phoenix only six or seven times. For one thing, she trusted the expertise of the professionals who were shooting the film. She also didn't want to spend too much of the school year, when the movie was being filmed, away from Solomon. And in truth, she thought the whole process was boring. "When you see how many times they shoot one scene, over and over and over again," she said, "you know one of them is right. I would say to Forest, 'Didn't you like that one? Didn't you think it was perfect?' Next thing you know, they have to do the scene again. . . . It was just so tedious!"

Terry still hadn't recovered from her personal losses, and writing *A Day Late and a Dollar Short* seemed impossible. While the book wasn't about her mother, the similarities between the ages and experiences of the fictional character and her mother were so great that even thinking about what the fictional character might do brought Terry too many painful memories. Then on April 10, Diane Cleaver, Terry's first agent, died in her Manhattan apartment at the age of 53. While her relationship with Diane had never been as close as her relationship to her mother or to Doris Jean, knowing yet another woman who had died in her fifties added to the weight of Terry's grief.

By the time the shooting of *Waiting to Exhale* finished in May, Terry was ready to go on the first vacation she had ever taken. She had always been so busy writing, promoting, caring for her family, and surviving, that she'd never taken time out to relax. After the stresses and losses of the previous 18 months, Terry understood that she needed to take some time for herself. She certainly didn't have the emotional energy to produce any creative work, and she also recognized that there were no guarantees. Only 43 herself, she had seen women dying well before old age. She suddenly realized, "Life is really short, too short. My girlfriend wasn't even 50 and my mother was 59 when she died. I was thinking . . . if I blink, I'll be 59. And I don't want to be one of these 'wish I coulda, woulda, shoulda.'"

So in June, Terry and producer Deborah Schindler, whom Terry had met on the set of *Waiting to Exhale*, went to Jamaica. Terry decided to experience the best the island had to offer. She went to the Grand Lido resort, which promised "the ultimate luxury vacation with superb accommodations and personalized service." The price included a luxurious suite with beachfront and garden views, all meals, land and water sports complete with personalized instructions and equipment rental, two miles of private white sand beach, and entertainment. No tipping was allowed. Deborah returned to the States, but Terry stayed on. Because the peak tourist season is in winter and early spring, she didn't feel crowded. She jogged along the beach, felt the sun and the breeze, and began to relax. "I felt my mother's spirit close by," she said, "and she told me to take happiness in the form in which it comes. She encouraged me to be receptive."

It was then that she met Jonathan Plummer, a six-foot-four man with dark wavy hair, a slight goatee, and huge eyes. Twenty-four-year-old Jonathan had no idea that Terry was a famous writer, but he did know that he was attracted to the older woman. The Plummers were a well-to-do, established family in Jamaica. They had wanted Jonathan to either become a doctor or take up some aspect of the management of their sugar estate. Instead, Jonathan was interested in the resort business. He was working at the nearby Sandals Resort when he met Terry.

At first, Terry was bothered by the 19-year difference in their ages. "I couldn't believe I actually liked someone his age," she confessed later. But then she started reconsidering the issue. "I never in a million years would have dreamed—I've never been out with a younger man before," she said, "but I really like him and he likes me, and then I started thinking about this whole double standard that men have been doing this for years and nobody says anything about it."

She also enjoyed being appreciated for who she is as a person, not what she has done or how much money she has earned. "The beauty of dealing with Jonathan," she explained, "is that he didn't even know who I was, and he didn't even care. He's so untarnished that all he knew was that he liked me. And even after he found out who I was, he still liked me."

The relationship totally rejuvenated Terry. "Inside of me, my entire being was singing. As I was walking along the beach," she remembered, "I said, 'Mama, you did this, didn't you?' I said it out loud. Then my cheeks started hurting because I was trying not to laugh, and I was giggling and stuff. And

Whoopi Goldberg and Angela Bassett in How Stella Got Her Groove Back. *Like many of Terry's books, this one is based on her own experiences. While in Jamaica recovering from her mother's death, Terry met a younger man, Jonathan Plummer, and fell in love.*

that's when I started thinking, particularly when I got home, *Mama sent him to me*, because this is the first time since she's been gone that I felt like myself. Like the person I really am. I think my mother said, 'It's time.'"

Terry returned to California a changed woman. Friends immediately noticed the difference, and when they heard her story, they told her she should send a ticket to Jonathan and fly him to California. Instead, she worked through her experience on paper, as she had so many times before. "Gradually I started feeling like myself again, and ended up writing a book about how you lose your spirit and what you have to give up to get it back," she explained.

Gone was the writer's block she had experienced when trying to work on *A Day Late and a Dollar Short*. This story flew off the keyboard. She began writing the book on September 6, 1995, and finished the first draft on September 30, just three weeks later. *How Stella Got Her Groove Back* is told from the perspective of Stella Payne, a 42-year-old investment analyst with an 11-year-old son from a marriage that ended in divorce. When her son visits his dad for a few weeks, Stella decides to take off on a vacation at a luxury resort in the Caribbean. There she meets Winston Shakespeare, a six-foot-four man half her age.

The parallels between Terry's life and the book are obvious, but she insists it isn't strictly autobiographical. "Stella isn't a reinvention of myself," she said in an interview with *Village Voice*. "She's only part of my persona. I can't believe people actually think my life is like that. What I give [my characters] are my concerns, which for the most part are grounded in reality."

Then, too, the fictional Winston Shakespeare is not a carbon copy of Jonathan Plummer. "First of all," Terry said in an interview with *People*, "Jonathan is not a hunk." And unlike Winston, a hotel chef, "Jonathan can't cook at all," Terry said in an interview with *Ebony*.

Terry sent the manuscript off to her publisher, Viking. The editors were expecting a book about a mother's struggles. Instead they got a romance between a woman in her forties and a 20-something young man at a luxury resort. The editors were surprised, but they bought the manuscript. Terry was paid a seven-figure advance. (Later, at the Medgar Evers College black writers conference, she said that at the time she was being paid $6 million per book.)

The book was scheduled to be released in May 1996 with a first printing of 800,000 hardcover copies. No novel written by an African American had ever been given that large a first printing.

Once her manuscript was off, Terry contacted Jonathan and invited him to join her and Solomon in California. He came on a student visa in October and enrolled at the local public community college to take courses in hotel management. She also gave him some money. "When I got paid a gazillion bucks for writing *Stella* . . . I felt like he should share in the cash," she said, "because without him I would never have written it. I just gave him a token, which just blew his mind.

He sent it back to Jamaica and invested it, but he lives off some of it." Terry didn't expect the relationship with Jonathan to become permanent, but she was determined to enjoy the moment.

Her relationship with Jonathan and the completion of *Stella* wasn't all Terry had to celebrate in 1995. On Christmas weekend, the movie *Waiting to Exhale* opened nationwide. Mostly African-American women lined up to see the movie the weekend it opened, pushing it to number one at the box office. They could identify with the four women in Terry's story. Once again, public reception of Terry's work shocked the experts. "When the [executives at Twentieth Century Fox] found out we were No. 1, they were trying to figure out, 'How can we reach a white audience, because the movie isn't playing real well in white communities,'" Terry reported. "My point is that you really don't get it, do you? This is about black people."

Waiting to Exhale ultimately grossed $67 million. The soundtrack hit number one on the music charts as well. No one had expected a movie based on the writings of an African-American woman to be so commercially successful. As Jack E. White observed in *Time* magazine, "*Exhale* demonstrates that it is no longer necessary for a book or movie to be targeted for whites to be a smash. The black audience alone can make it one."

Alice Walker, whose novel *The Color Purple* had been the last adaptation of an African-American woman's writing to reach the big screen, praised Terry's work. While she didn't share Terry's view of life, she supported her right to portray the world the way she saw it. "Whether or not Terry McMillan should have written this or made a movie of it or whatever—of course she should have," Walker said in an interview with the online magazine *Salon*. "This is how she sees life. She is an artist and she should be supported in her view. I hope that people

Terry invited Jonathan Plummer to join her and Solomon in Danville in 1995. Shortly thereafter, he would experience life with a celebrity with the opening of the movie version of Waiting to Exhale *and the release of the book* How Stella Got Her Groove Back.

are more understanding and less eager to trash than they were ten years ago."

Terry was grateful for such words from a revered figure in African-American literary circles. In spite of her commercial success, she generally felt ignored or underappreciated by African-American intellectuals. Publisher Max Rodriguez, pleased by the success of black authors such as Terry, lamented in his publication *Quarterly Black Review,* "Where is the literature? Where are the seminal pieces that mark the passage of time in the life of a people? Where are the Langston Hugheses, the Ellisons, the Wrights, the Hurstons, and the Hansberrys?"

Part of Terry's problem was that a group of African-American intellectuals wanted black fiction to deal with issues between blacks and whites in American society and her novels didn't do that. "I don't write about victims," she proclaimed. "They just bore me to death. I prefer to write about somebody who can pick themselves back up and get on with their lives. Because all of us are victims to some extent."

Another side to the problem was much more personal. Terry craved direct affirmation from her literary idols. Maya Angelou, the celebrated African-American poet, wrote to Terry, "You're one good,

good writing sister," but Alice Walker and Toni Morrison made no personal contact with her. They did not write blurbs for the jackets of her novels, which Terry interpreted as a failure to show support.

A more significant failing from Terry's perspective was Alice Walker's reaction to a question Terry asked at a children's book party where Walker was giving a reading of her children's book *Finding the Green Stone*. The question dealt with Walker's novel *Possessing the Secret of Joy*, which has adult themes. Feeling a discussion about such topics would be inappropriate while surrounded by young children, Walker simply said, "That's true," and moved on to another topic. Terry assumed she was being snubbed and mentioned the incident in a number of interviews.

In 1997, Alice Walker gave an indirect piece of advice to Terry in the form of the essay "This That I Offer You" which appeared in Walker's book *Anything We Love Can Be Saved*. Giving Terry the pseudonym "Anna Caday," Walker addressed some of her criticisms and then raised the question, "What can we do about the needs others have of us that we, being human and therefore limited and imperfect, cannot fulfill?"

Walker went on to talk about the correspondence she'd had with Langston Hughes when she was in her early twenties. When at one point he didn't respond to an urgent letter from her, she thought he was either angry or disappointed in her. A week or so later, she learned that he had died. "We must learn to accept, as I had to then," she concluded, "that people get tired, cross, overworked, and overextended. . . . If they are well known, they get more stuff in the mail than they can possibly read or respond to. . . . They get sick and sometimes they die. And none of it has anything, really, to do with us, and what we need or expect from them."

Terry's response to the essay isn't known, but later interviews she gave didn't seem to include as many complaints about lack of respect and attention from other African-American writers.

Perhaps with her busy schedule and fame, Terry began to better understand the limitations Morrison and Walker lived with. Not only was Terry continuing to write, but she spoke at writers' conferences, bookstores, college writing classes, and workshops for screenwriters. She had a house built in Danville, California, and once again went through the process of moving. In January 1996, she established the Doris Jean Austin Fellowships for African-American Fiction Writers to honor the memory of her friend, and then she went on another long book tour, this time publicizing the April 1996 release of *How Stella Got Her Groove Back*. Jonathan Plummer went with her and got his first exposure to just what a celebrity Terry had become.

A movie based on the book was soon in the works, and once again Terry worked with Ron Bass to write the screenplay. The movie was released on August 14, 1998, and starred Angela Bassett as Stella, Whoopi Goldberg as Stella's friend Delilah, and newcomer Taye Diggs as Winston. One joke in the movie connected Haiti with a high incidence of AIDS cases, and this stirred up protest both in the nation of Haiti and among Haitian Americans. As a result, Twentieth Century Fox removed the line from the home video version of the film.

After the movie's release, Terry returned to a schedule of writing at home interspersed with speaking engagements at far-flung places. September 1998 found her on the island of Maui, speaking at the annual Maui Writers Conference. When she appeared to make her Sunday evening presentation September 6, she had a surprise for everyone. The day before, she and Jonathan Plummer got married on a nearby Maui beach. Solomon, Terry's sister Crystal, and a niece and nephew attended the ceremony.

Terry occasionally reads excerpts from *A Day Late and a Dollar Short* at speaking engagements, which was released in January of 2001 by Viking Press. But if she never publishes another word, she already has revolutionized the publishing industry. Before Terry McMillan arrived on the scene, publishers refused to recognize that middle-class African Americans would buy books. They did not know how to make use of existing avenues within the African-American community for distributing such books. And they did not understand that the African-American experience is made up of more than poverty and discrimination. Terry forced those publishers to see that by denying the broader humanity of the African-American experience, they were literally losing millions of dollars in sales revenues. As Ken Smikle, publisher of *Target Market News*, a trade magazine about black consumers, said, Terry has been "dragging the industry kicking and screaming into what has become a very lucrative situation." And with the unexpected success of *Waiting to Exhale*, she also changed the way Hollywood looks at "black" movies.

From the time she was a child, Terry McMillan has been determined not to let anyone else shape her destiny. She has refused to let the way things have always been become an excuse for refusing to change. Because of that commitment, she has carved out a better world for herself and for the new generation of novelists and screenwriters who have been following her.

CHRONOLOGY

———— ❧ ————

1951	Terry McMillan is born on October 18 to MadelineWashington McMillan and Edward Lewis McMillan in Port Huron, Michigan.
1963	Terry's parents divorce.
1966	Takes job at Port Huron Public Library; discovers African-American writers.
1969	Terry's father dies from complications of diabetes and alcoholism; Terry graduates from high school and moves to Los Angeles.
1970	Begins classes at Los Angeles City College.
1971	Writes first poem and sees it published.
1973	Transfers to the University of California at Berkeley and moves to the San Francisco Bay area.
1976	Graduates from Berkeley.
1979	Moves to New York City and enrolls in Columbia University School of Fine Arts to begin work on her master's degree.
1981	Leaves Columbia; works as temporary typist at various Manhattan law firms; quits using cocaine.
1982	Meets Leonard Welch, who later moves in with her; earns residency at Yaddo Writers' Colony.
1983	Attends Alcoholics Anonymous meetings and quits drinking alcohol; attends Yaddo again as well as the MacDowell Colony; joins Harlem Writers Guild; discovers she is pregnant.
1984	Solomon Welch, Terry's son, is born on April 24.
1985	Breaks off relationship with Leonard Welch; submits *Mama* to Houghton Mifflin and is given a contract.
1986	Becomes a one-woman publicity firm, sending out more than 4,000 letters to publicize upcoming release of *Mama*.
1987	*Mama* is released on January 15; the first printing of 5,000 copies is already sold out; moves to Laramie, Wyoming, to accept one-year teaching position at the University of Wyoming; begins work on *Breaking Ice: An Anthology of Contemporary African-American Fiction*.

1988	Moves to Tucson, Arizona, to accept position as associate professor at the University of Arizona; gets contract with Penguin for *Disappearing Acts*.
1989	*Disappearing Acts* is released in August.
1990	Defamation lawsuit filed on behalf of Leonard Welch against Terry and her publishers in August; *Breaking Ice* is published; begins work on *Waiting to Exhale*; serves on National Book Award committee for fiction.
1991	Takes leave of absence from University of Arizona after spring term; Leonard Welch's lawsuit is dismissed; moves to California.
1992	Movie rights for *Waiting to Exhale* sold to Twentieth Century Fox; the book is released in May; goes on six-week book tour; *Waiting to Exhale* sells 800,000 hardcover copies before paperback version released; Terry works on screenplay for movie.
1993	Madeline Tillman, Terry's mother, dies in September.
1994	Best friend Doris Jean Austin dies in September.
1995	Shooting of movie *Waiting to Exhale* begins in February; Terry goes on vacation to Jamaica in June; meets Jonathan Plummer and is rejuvenated; returns to California and writes first draft of *How Stella Got Her Groove Back* in three weeks; Jonathan joins Terry in California; *Waiting to Exhale* released in theaters on Christmas weekend and is number one at the box office.
1996	*How Stella Got Her Groove Back* is released in May with a record-breaking first printing of 800,000 hardcover copies; accompanied by Jonathan Plummer, Terry goes on book tour.
1997	Works on screenplay for *How Stella Got Her Groove Back*.
1998	*How Stella Got Her Groove Back* released in theaters in August; marries Jonathan Plummer on September 5 while at a conference in Maui.
2001	*A Day Late and A Dollar Short* published by Viking.

BIBLIOGRAPHY

Blythe, William. "Hustling for Dignity." *New York Times*, February 22, 1987, sect. 7.

Bowling, Anne. "Terry McMillan: 'Everything I Write Is About Empowerment.'" From *1999 Writer's Yearbook,* reprinted at *http://writersdigest.com/newsletter/mcmillan2*.

Fein, Esther B. "Fiction Vérité: Womanish Talk That's Quoted Chapter and Verse." *New York Times*, July 1, 1992, sect. C.

Fisk, Alan. "From Baseball 'Memories' to Self-help to 'Junk Literature,' Writers Had It All." *Detroit News*, May 20, 1997; reprinted at *http://detnews.com/1997/accent/9705/20/0520028*.

Hubbard, Kim, and Penelope Rowlands. "On Top of Her Game." *People*, April 29, 1996.

Hunter, Jeffrey W., Deborah A. Schmitt, and Timothy J. White, eds. *Contemporary Literary Criticism,* vol. 112. Farmington Hills, MI: Gale Research, 1999.

Janis, Pam. "The Stories of Her Life: Terry McMillan's Groove Is Women with Strength." *Detroit News*, May 10, 1997.

Jones, Daniel, and John D. Jorgenson, ed. *Contemporary Authors: New Revision Series,* vol. 60. Detroit, MI: Gale Research, 1998.

Leland, John. "How Terry Got Her Groove." *Newsweek*, April 29, 1996.

Matuz, Roger, ed. *Contemporary Literary Criticism,* vol. 61. Detroit, MI: Gale Research, 1990.

Max, Daniel. "McMillan's Millions." *New York Times Magazine*, August 9, 1992, sect. 6.

McMillan, Terry. Paper delivered at the "Writing the Southwest" conference, cited at University of New Mexico website: *http://www.unm.edu/~wrtgsw/mcmillan*.

_____. *Mama*. Boston: Houghton Mifflin, 1987.

_____. *Waiting to Exhale*. New York: Pocket Books, 1992.

_____. "Publicizing Your Novel." In *The Writer as Publicist*. New York: Poets & Writers, 1993.

_____. "This Is America." In Haki R. Madhubuti, ed., *Why L.A. Happened: Implications of the '92 Los Angeles Rebellion*. Chicago: Third World Press, 1993.

Norment, Lynn. "Waiting to Exhale." *Ebony*, December 1995.

Patrick, Diane. *Terry McMillan: The Unauthorized Biography*. New York: St. Martin's Press, 1999.

Randolph, Laura B. "Terry McMillan Exhales and Inhales in a Revealing Interview." *Ebony*, May 1993.

Richards, Paulette. *Terry McMillan: A Critical Companion*, Critical Companions to Popular Contemporary Writers. Westport, CT: Greenwood Publishing, 1999.

Sellers, Frances Stead. "Terry McMillan: *Waiting to Exhale*." *Times Literary Supplement*, November 6, 1992.

Sheldon, Michael. "How Terry Trained Her Own Mr. Right." *Electronic Telegraph*, September 28, 1996, at http://www.telegraph.co.uk/et?ac=002082058247883&rtmo=aNX8J w3L&atmo.../tlmen28.

Skow, John. "Some Groove." *Time*, May 6, 1996.

"'Stella' In South Africa: Still Looking for Her Groove." *Ebony*, December 1996.

Walker, Alice. *Anything We Love Can Be Saved: A Writer's Activism*. New York: Ballantine, 1997.

White, Jack E. "Heavy Breathing." *Time*, January 15, 1996.

Wilkerson, Isabel. "On Top of the World." *Essence*, June 1996.

BOOKS BY TERRY MCMILLAN

INDEX

PICTURE CREDITS

BRUCE AND BECKY DUROST FISH are freelance writers and editors who have worked on more than 100 books for children and young adults. They have degrees in history and literature and live on the high desert of Central Oregon. The Fishes have written more than a dozen books for Chelsea House.